# RISE
# OF THE
# SUPER FURRY
# ANIMALS

RISE
OF THE
SUPER FURRY
ANIMALS

# RISE OF THE SUPER FURRY ANIMALS

### RIC RAWLINS

THE FRIDAY PROJECT

The Friday Project
An imprint of HarperCollins*Publishers*
1 London Bridge Street
London SE1 9GF

www.harpercollins.co.uk

Published by The Friday Project 2015

1

Copyright © Ric Rawlins

Ric Rawlins asserts the moral right to be identified as the author of this work

A catalogue record for this book is available from the British Library

ISBN 978-0-00-810523-5

Typeset by Palimpsest Book Production Limited, Falkirk, Stirlingshire
Printed in Great Britain by Clays Ltd, St Ives plc

All rights reserved. No part of this publication may be reproduced, stored in a retrieval system, or transmitted, in any form or by any means, electronic, mechanical, photocopying, recording or otherwise, without the prior written permission of the publishers.

**MIX**
Paper from
responsible sources
FSC
www.fsc.org  **FSC C007454**

FSC™ is a non-profit international organisation established to promote the responsible management of the world's forests. Products carrying the FSC label are independently certified to assure consumers that they come from forests that are managed to meet the social, economic and ecological needs of present and future generations, and other controlled sources.

Find out more about HarperCollins and the environment at
**www.harpercollins.co.uk/green**

To Marianne and Acorn

# CONTENTS

Author's Note   xi
Dramatis Personae   xiii
Prologue   1

Chapter One   9
Mountain lessons / Hot Puke / The pirates of
Bethesda / Citizens band

Chapter Two   19
Festival time / The wildest man in North
Wales / Heavy metal hoax / Ffa Coffi Pawb

Chapter Three   31
Ankst Records / Gorky's Zygotic Mynci /
Why aren't we making techno? / The long walk home

Chapter Four   37
The teacher / Rock and squat / Cardiff
in the sun / The rave

Chapter Five                                                51
SFA Soundsystem / The man don't give
a dub / Rhys says adios / Into space

Chapter Six                                                 59
Birth of a ringtone / London turns
on / Moog Droog / The wisdom of
Robert Plant / Outlaw aircraft carrier

Chapter Seven                                               69
Tour of Cornwall / The number 23 / Fuzzy Birds /
Outlaw hunting / Something out of Killing Joke

Chapter Eight                                               79
Fired from a cannon / Hanging with Howard
Marks / Meet the press / Baz

Chapter Nine                                                91
Turning Japanese / F-16 Jetstreams / Cian-do
attitude / Off the map

Chapter Ten                                                101
Painting demons / Bouncy castle licence /
S4C on the attack / Overtaken by a wheel

Chapter Eleven                                             113
Rise of the Shinto gods / Air panic / Gringos in
the mist / Unbridled freedom

Chapter Twelve                                             125
Deep sleep earthquake / Big trouble in Bogotá /
Death to the monarchy

Chapter Thirteen                                          133
William Hague's letter / Ice hockey hootenanny /
Britpop turbulence / Electric harps

Chapter Fourteen                                          143
Taekwondo music / Love letter to El Niño /
Das Koolies

Chapter Fifteen                                           153
Placid Casual, Acid Casuals / Bear in a vice /
Gods and monsters

Chapter Sixteen                                           161
Kamikaze at Glastonbury / Bouncy ghetto
blaster / Mash it up / Creation goes down

Chapter Seventeen                                         171
Recovered histories / The Roman road / Smoking
goats / Pop strike / America

Chapter Eighteen                                          183
East coast negotiations / Lost in time

Chapter Nineteen                                          189
Intermission / Experiments with earthquakes /
The Skull God / Furrymania / Yeti psychosis

Chapter Twenty                                            199
Wasteland Gods / Travels in a space buggy /
Pizza trippin'

Epilogue                                                  207

# AUTHOR'S NOTE

With the band's consent – and hopefully not too much distress from anyone I've forgotten to ask – some of the sections in this book have been 'cinematised': that is to say, scripted up and CGI'd into narrative-friendly shape. That said, everything you're about to read is based on the subjective truth of interviews taken during the research process. It's also worth noting that, although this is a book in the English language, many of the conversations replicated here – particularly those spoken by the band – would have originally taken place in what Gruff describes as a 'cracked youthful version' of the Welsh language.

# DRAMATIS PERSONAE

### SUPER FURRY ANIMALS

Cian Ciaran
Dafydd Ieuan
Gruff Rhys
Guto Pryce
Huw Bunford

### FFA COFFI PAWB

Gruff Rhys
Dafydd Ieuan
Rhodri Puw
Dewi Emlyn

### WALES MOVERS AND SHAKERS

Gorwel Owen
Record producer

Rhys Mwyn
Founder, Anhrefn and Recordiau Anhrefn

Dafydd Rhys
Brother of Gruff Rhys, founder of Pesda Roc festival

Emyr Williams
Co-founder, Ankst Records

Rhys Ifans
Actor, fanzine writer, Super Furry Animal

LONDON MOVERS AND SHAKERS

Brian Cannon
Photographer, filmmaker and creator of imagery

Alan McGee
The boss, Creation Records

John Andrews
Marketing manager, Creation Records

Dick Green
Super Furry Animals representative, Creation Records

Andy Saunders
Press officer, Creation Records

Ian Mahoney
SFA tour manager 1995–8

# PROLOGUE

There, blinking in the darkness, were five shaggy-haired individuals in dressing gowns. The Super Furry Animals had woken up in a rural cottage at four in the morning, with only half-remembered instructions to help themselves to coffee. As they all sat around a large oak table, the one with dark hair suddenly flopped onto its surface with a primeval groan. He was shaken awake again.

A sixth man swaggered in wearing only boxer shorts, smoking a pipe and ticking off the final checklists from his notebook. His name was Ian Mahoney. He was the tour manager.

'Right!' clapped Mahoney, joining his comrades at the table. 'This is where we are.'

He placed a cornflake over a small village in South Wales called Penybanc.

'And John is waiting for us on the farm . . . over here.'

He placed another cornflake two centimetres below.

'John has got the armed vehicle. We will rendezvous with him at 0600 hours – which gives us one hour – then we will mount the vehicle and drive across here . . .' he slid the cornflake north, 'and the festival is over *here*!' It landed over a small village called Llandeilo. 'Any questions?'

The singer tilted his head like a curious dog.

'Good. Now let's go! Go! Go!'

It was getting light as their car skidded up the muddy banks of the farm. The kitchen lights blinked on, then John Andrews of Creation Records stepped out of the cottage in a dressing gown, pulling it over his head to avoid the drizzle. He smiled into the headlights and waved the car along through a small flock of sheep.

The car finally parked in the corner of a field, twenty feet away from another vehicle: this one considerably larger, and covered by tarpaulins. John cackled to himself and threw some wellies on, then trudged over to greet the band.

'Glad you could make it,' he said, fist-pumping them one by one. 'The beast is waiting patiently!'

'Good to hear it, John! Do you think the media suspect anything?' asked tour manager Ian.

'I've not heard a whisper, Ian, and I don't expect to – at least until we reach the A4.' He suddenly looked quite thoughtful. 'Then we will probably be arrested.'

Twenty miles away in a huge green field, the annual National Eisteddfod was creaking into action. Tents were being raised, harps were being tuned, and the sun was shimmering through the bright blue sky.

The Eisteddfod festival is said to have its origins in the druidic rites of the twelfth century, and its stated purpose is to turn artists into bards, under the judgement of the Arch Druid. Renowned as a patriotic event, the Eisteddfod enforces a Welsh-language-only policy for its artists, and on this particular day, it was enforcing the policy in the fields of Llandeilo.

Down by the side of the main stage, a television crew dressed in Hawaiian shirts were interviewing the festival's spokesperson.

'So what can we expect from today's festivities?' asked the young presenter, grinning through his sunglasses.

'Well, as usual the Eisteddfod festival will be priding itself on the very best in Welsh-language arts and entertainment,' said the spokesperson, 'plus, hopefully we will be anointing some bards into the druidic order, which – as you know – dates back centuries.'

'And what do you make of the controversial decision to invite the Super Furry Animals to play?'

The spokesperson's eyes misted over, as if he had detected a subtle change in temperature. 'The Super Furry Animals? Well, of course they are a matter of national pride too. And what's more, we're delighted to have them!'

'But haven't they been known to sing in English on occasion?'

The spokesperson folded his arms. 'The Super Furries will be on their best, Welsh-speaking behaviour today. I can assure you of that!'

Eight miles away, the army tank rolled over the hill. Attached to its missile turret were twin speakers pumping out a steady techno groove. The tank had been painted bright psychedelic blue, with thick yellow letters spelling out a simple question above its headlights: 'A OES HEDDWCH?'[1]

The manhole lid flipped open and Gruff appeared, squinting through the sun at the tents on the far horizon. The techno was loud up on top, and it seemed to phase left and right according to the direction of the wind. 'Festival wind!' he thought, making a mental note of this strange audio phenomenon.

Down below, his bandmate Cian was cueing up 'Sail On Sailor' by the Beach Boys on the decks, while Daf tapped his drumsticks

---

[1] 'Is There Peace?'

against the gun controls, raising nervous eyebrows. The other band members sat in the darkness, dimly lit by flickering neon light.

'It's fucking dehumanising down here!' shouted Guto over the tumbling noise of the engine.

'What do you mean?' yelled Daf.

'Well, it's pretty cramped, isn't it? – I keep banging my head!'

Daf lit a cigar and leaned into Guto's ear. 'They are pretty cramped,' he yelled, 'but at least they scare the shit out of the other cars!'

John and Ian of Creation Records were in the front compartment – and feeling increasingly uneasy. In the far distance they'd noticed a police van parked by the festival gates, and John had begun impulsively stroking his chin.

'Let's not do anything to make them feel nervous,' he said.

'Such as driving up to them with a military-grade weapon?' asked Ian.

'Mmm,' said John.

Ian stopped the tank, looked again at the map, then made an announcement. 'Well I think we're going the wrong way anyway. Take a look at this.' He sprawled the map onto John's knees and pointed at the festival region. It showed that although they were heading for the main gate, the artists' field was significantly closer: two fields to their right.

'That's interesting,' said John. 'Can we turn around?'

Half a mile ahead, a small group of police officers were starting to hear traces of the Beach Boys in the air. One security officer stepped forwards, looked through a pair of binoculars, and began muttering obscenities.

'I can't turn around, John, there's traffic all around us,' said Ian.

'Well . . . we'll just have to drive up to the police then. Maybe they'll be nice. In fact, I have definitely heard that the police are nice around here.'

As John said those last words, a strange smell began leaking into their compartment. Ian looked confused for a second, then suddenly terrified – as a trickle of smoke wafted up his nose. John jumped up and pulled back the curtains, but he couldn't see the passengers: the dope smoke was too thick.

'Holy mother of Moses,' uttered John.

Up the road, the Celtic harp recital was just beginning. Lime cordial was being served, while the festival spokesperson stood to the side of the stage, preparing to make his final TV appearance of the day.

'Ah, those lovely harps,' he sighed. 'Did you know that this festival dates back to the druidic ceremonies of the twelfth century?'

'Yes, I had heard something about that,' smiled the presenter. 'Right – shall we begin the filming then?'

'Hang on!' interrupted the spokesperson. He narrowed his eyes, as if sensing a distant threat. Then he whispered: 'What is that terrible noise?'

The rumble seemed to almost come from deep underground, but then it turned aggressive, feral. An old man sat in his deckchair began bleating and waving his stick in the air. The spokesperson chewed his fingernails. Then it dawned on him what the noise was: 'The Beach Boys!'

The tank was rumbling downhill at quite a slow speed, but it was also shaking uncontrollably as it hit all the bumps in the field. Behind it was the brown gate. The brown gate was good. Ahead of it was the blue gate, though – and nobody quite knew what the blue gate was all about. Ian and John started babbling.

'Look!' shouted John. 'A gap in the hedge – straight ahead!'

Ian squinted at the hedge. 'That's not a gap!'

'It's the field we need, Ian. Head towards it, just head towards it . . .'

He put one hand on the wheel.

'Get off my wheel! Look at your eyes – you've got the eyes of a madman!'

They burst through the hedge, slammed up a steep incline, and stopped. The tank stood motionless for a few seconds, silent except for the sound of gently creaking metal and a cool breeze.

Inside, Cian lit a match. 'Rats,' he muttered, lifting a vinyl to the light and tracing a scratch with his finger. After a quick check to see if everyone was OK, Gruff lifted the hatch and peered out. Looking across the field, he could see a big tent at the far side, with the sign 'ARTISTS' ENTRANCE' next to it. He looked back down into the tank, where the quiet sneeze of laughter had overcome his bandmates.

'I think we're in the correct field,' he announced.

The rest of the day panned out well for the festival: bards were appointed, ale was drunk, eighteenth-century costumes were worn, and the tank finally found its home – in a field where teenagers could boogie to Cian's techno.

Later in the evening, the festival spokesperson wandered down to the stage where Super Furry Animals were playing. He slurped on a ginger ale while tapping his feet and humming along. One thing seemed curious, however: the crowd were singing along to an instrumental performance. Stranger still, although some were singing in Welsh, others were singing in English and . . . was that even *Japanese* he heard? He walked into the audience and spotted a girl handing out lyric sheets.

'Would you mind if I took a look at this?' he smiled, grabbing a pamphlet. At the top of the first page was an illustration of a dragon screwing a man up the arse, while the lyrics below were printed in a variety of translations, a different one on each page. Finally, a simple instruction: 'SING ALONG IN WHICHEVER LANGUAGE YOU LIKE'. The spokesperson put his quivering hand over his mouth, then looked back at the stage.

The contradiction of voices as they blended into one another made for an almighty sound – indecipherable, certainly – but also a strange kind of international language.

# CHAPTER I
## MOUNTAIN LESSONS / HOT PUKE / THE PIRATES OF BETHESDA / CITIZENS BAND

It was a misty morning in 1974, and four-year-old Gruff Rhys was being carried up the side of a mountain, perched on his dad's shoulders. Once they'd reached a level where they could see the valley before them, his father put him down and pointed up to where the rocks hit the mist.

'That, Gruff, is the peak of the mountain!'

Gruff nodded.

'Unfortunately, my lad, the peak of the mountain is the most boring part. But! Take a look over there, at the dip between the rocks. Do you see?'

He pointed slightly further down, to where a pathway seemed to wind its way cryptically between the hills before disappearing round the corner.

'Those are the passes – the gateways *between* the mountains!'

Gruff nodded.

'It's along those passes that you'll find different peoples meeting and interacting with each other. Historically they are a link between cultures . . . a connection between the towns.' He put his son back on his shoulders and set off again.

'It's not the peaks of the mountains that matter, lad,' he announced. 'It's the gaps between them!'

Gruff's family had recently moved to the slate-quarrying town of Bethesda from Cardiff. This had mainly been because Gruff's dad had taken a job as county secretary in nearby Caernarfon, but Bethesda also appealed because it was a Welsh-speaking area.

'My grandfather had lost the Welsh language by one generation,' says Gruff today, 'so my father spoke English with him and Welsh with his mother – and could never imagine speaking to either of them in any other language.'

By contrast, both Gruff's parents spoke to him, his brother and his sister in Welsh: the family was going back to its roots.

Gruff's father, Ioan Bowen Rees, had two main passions: he was a committed public servant, and he loved the Welsh mountains. The two themes came together in the books that he wrote, in which the freedom of the mountains provided a convenient metaphor for his political philosophy. Ioan was widely regarded as a fair man who could rise above petty political games, a left-wing internationalist who disregarded the obsessive self-worship of his country as insularism. His politics were forged during an era of social tension and cold war propaganda, and he shared his thoughts openly, telling one interviewer that 'the battle for Wales is the battle for *all* small nations, all small communities, all individuals in the age of genocide'.

Gruff's mother, Margaret, ran the local Welsh-language playgroup. She was also a teacher who shared her husband's love of writing, and had composed a book of poems. According to Gruff, 'She did one book, a book of sonnets. If I remember correctly most sonnets have fourteen lines, but she specialised in thirteen-line sonnets.'

At home, the music on the stereo was a curious mixture. Ioan was a record collector who despised pop, instead preferring the 'proper music' of composers such as Wagner, who'd be blasted from the speakers at full volume. And yet, strangely enough, reggae was deemed acceptable, as was Welsh-language pop. National radio stations such as Radio One were cut off by the mountains surrounding Bethesda, but Gruff and his siblings found other ways of discovering international pop music: the frequencies of Irish stations would occasionally travel across the sea, transmitting the disco hits of the 1970s alongside the occasional Celtic fiddle ballad.

At the age of six, Gruff learned that Planet Earth was about to come to an abrupt end. One day, he and his cousin returned home from messing about in the fields to discover a book that Gruff's brother had left lying about. 'TIME AND THE GALAXY', boomed the title. Flicking through the pages, their curiosity turned to morbid horror as they came across an illustration of the sun crashing into Earth, melting human civilisation into a pool of lava in the process. Underneath was a simple caption: 'The fate of the sun.' Understandably, the kids were devastated.

'At this time we hadn't even realised that our parents were going to die,' says Gruff, 'so we were completely terrified at the thought of this massive event. Unfortunately we didn't read the book any further, so we were oblivious to the fact that it wouldn't happen for a really long time.'

## FURRY FILE: GRUFF

BORN – Hwlffordd, 1970 ('In the hospital')
CHILDHOOD SUPERPOWER – Hallucination
CHILDHOOD SUPERWEAKNESS – Pasties
CHILDHOOD DISASTER – 'I had a ticket to see Gary Moore and Phil Lynott at the Manchester Apollo, when I was thirteen. And my parents decided I shouldn't go to Manchester on my

> own at thirteen to watch a heavy metal band . . . and then Phil Lynott died a few weeks after. That was a bit of a scar'
> CHILDHOOD VICTORY – Discovering music ('It was a defining change of pace')
> BAD BEHAVIOUR – Covering school books with cartoons. 'I got a detention, then didn't turn up to that, then I got detained for a whole term . . . based on a cartoon'
> TEEN REBEL ICON – Lou Reed
> TEEN GROOMING TIP – Not grooming
> GEEKY PASSION – The Velvet Underground ('From the age of thirteen that was my specialist *Mastermind* subject')
> FIRST SONGWRITING ATTEMPT – 'Rydwi'n Mynd Yn Hén' ('It was about getting old . . . I was five')
> BEACH BOYS VALHALLA – 'Feel Flows'

Rock and roll education came early. Gruff's older brother Dafydd formed a band called Chwd Poeth, meaning 'Hot Puke', who were barred from performing at school after they'd apparently vomited on the audience at their first show. Inspired by such cavalier behaviour, Gruff began collecting plastic buckets to play the drums on, eventually finding one that sounded uncannily like a bass drum. Unfortunately the drummer from Chwd Poeth agreed, and stole it to use on stage himself.

One October morning, Gruff's school announced that the world's first Welsh-language horror film would be projected in the sports barn. *Gwaed Ar Y Sêr* ('Blood on the Stars') was about a group of choirboys who invited celebrities to their church then gruesomely slaughtered them. The nine-year-old kids screamed with delight at its gory scenes, although Gruff found himself more interested in the short film they screened afterwards to calm everyone down. It was a concert documentary about a popular 1970s Welsh group, called Edward H. Dafis. They were performing a grand farewell show – their last before breaking up for ever.

Gruff stared up at the flickering Super-8 images, and slowly grew more and more mesmerised by the peaceful acoustic meditations of the band. When the spool eventually ran out, he looked up and asked a teacher: 'Which of the music players was Edward H. Dafis, miss?'

'Ah, Gruff,' smiled the teacher. 'I don't think any of them are called that. That's just the name of the band!'

Impressed, Gruff decided that Edward H. Dafis were his favourite new band. However, this was to be short lived: the week after, they were replaced by another folk-rock group, Ac Eraill. 'They were like a boy band, but a folk boy band with long hair,' says Gruff today, describing them. The following week he discovered another band to add to his list of Great New Bands – and when he couldn't find another the week after, it was clearly time to form one himself.

That Saturday, Gruff's mum drove him to the youth club. A local teacher had come up with the idea of training kids to play rock, encouraging local groups to donate their old instruments in a co-operative scheme. The strategy was, at least in part, successful.

'We've got five drum kits and, er . . . well, we've got five drum kits,' said the man behind reception. 'Shall I put you down for drum lessons?'

After a few hours of bashing out crude rhythms, Gruff noticed another kid being dropped off outside. During the lunch break, Gruff would discover that his name was Daf, and that – coincidentally – he was also there for drum lessons.

'My dad took me to the club,' says Daf today. 'I didn't want to go because I was super shy at the time, so he forced me. On that first day Gruff and me started learning to play drums together. We were both twelve and lived about forty miles apart from each other.' Despite the distance, Gruff and Daf got on well enough to make a *Goonies*-style pact: they agreed that, should one of them ever need the other to play drums, they would be there.

In summer 1983, Gruff's brother attended a pirate radio conference in Birmingham. Upon returning home to Bethesda, his parents opened the door to find him armed to the teeth with illegal contraptions which, he said, would facilitate the pirate radio takeover of North Wales.

Within twenty-four hours, he'd recruited Gruff to the cause. Suddenly a strange combination of guitar-based jingles and *Python*-style sketches were being broadcast from the peaks of the mountains. This was, in fact, literally the case: the mountaintops provided the best signal for the transmitter, so Dafydd would scale them by night and hide the device among the rocks, sourcing the frequency so that they could operate from home.

There followed two weeks of successful broadcasting, until one night Dafydd burst through the door of his brother's room with a mildly disconcerting smile. 'We're on telly,' he panted.

The two of them jumped downstairs to catch the evening news, with Dafydd leaning so close the light flickered on his face.

'Tonight the police are engaged in a manhunt for the pirates of Bethesda: the illegal DJs who are transmitting on the exact same frequency used by the local police force . . . and causing mayhem.'

'Awesome!' Dafydd laughed. 'We've been broadcasting on the police frequency!'

He switched off the lights and crawled over to the window. Down in the night below, two police cars were projecting their headlights up the steep curves of the opposite mountain. 'They know the transmitter's up there,' whispered Dafydd.

The pirates' days were numbered, but Bethesda's underground radio scene was just getting started. Citizens band radio, or CB as it was commonly known, was a form of short-wave communication made famous by Hollywood movies during the 1970s. American truckers used CB to communicate in *Smokey and the Bandit*, while the cops in *The Dukes of Hazzard* used it to bark at each other while speeding through Kentucky. Now, for reasons that nobody could quite explain, the teenagers of Bethesda were using it to communicate between the valleys.

It was 1982.

'Your basic CB system is quite crude,' said the moustached man at the car boot sale, holding up two pieces of scrap metal to an audience of bewitched children. 'You just slot this bit into here . . . then plug this wire in here . . . then talk through this bit over here!' He burped. 'Excuse me, children. Now does anyone have any questions?'

'My father says it is illegal!' announced one kid.

'Well,' said the moustached man, leaning in with a glint in his teeth. 'I guess your father just ain't cool then, is he?'

Within weeks, CB was more popular than *ET*. As soon as night descended on the valleys, entire networks of teenagers began transmitting messages to one another, using codenames to protect their identities from the police. The police, meanwhile, would be stationed on the other end of town, listening in from their vans. As far as they could fathom, an underground criminal network had come to town; it would be some weeks before they realised it was just a bunch of kids.

Meanwhile, the codenames grew ever more mysterious: Gruff became known as 'Goblin', while the weediest kid in school renamed himself 'The Black Stallion'. It was communication chaos – a kind of primitive social network – and the more it continued, the more an interesting side effect emerged: since all the coded language had been inspired by truckers in American movies, a weird hybrid language began to develop that was part Hollywood bandit-speak, part Welsh tongue.

# CHAPTER 2

**FESTIVAL TIME /
THE WILDEST MAN IN NORTH WALES /
HEAVY METAL HOAX / FFA COFFI PAWB**

With the young people of Bethesda engaged in their social network experiment, it wasn't long before groups started linking together, joining the dots and forming new realities on the ground. One such manifestation was the emergence of a live music boom, organised almost entirely by left-wing political groups.

Cymdeithas yr Iaith Gymraeg (the Welsh Language Society) was the most prolific: their young activists put on gigs to raise cash and awareness for the miners who were being stung by the Thatcher government, while campaigning for equal status for the Welsh language. Their guerrilla activities included artfully manipulating English-language signs, in a cheeky style that would later become popular with organisations such as Adbusters. Their ideology was simple: 'non-violent, direct action'.

'Welsh-language culture back then was kind of an outsider thing – you were out there,' says Emyr Glyn Williams, co-founder of Ankst Records. 'Now obviously you can get a government grant for all sorts of things, but in that time the "living Welsh culture" was kind of free and independent, and it was based around things like the rock scene.'

The local CND group got involved in live music too, as did a collective of student promoters from the nearby university town of

Bangor. The result was a sudden cultural explosion which spawned a new generation of hedonistic, radical Welsh-language pop groups.

Gruff and his brother were smack bang in the middle of this melting pot. By 1984 the former had graduated from biscuit tins to full-sized drums and was playing in a band called Machlud. Meanwhile Dafydd was the manager of a local pop sensation: Maffia Mr Huws. Known as the fab five of North Wales, they inspired countless imitators with their commercial songs and healthy teeth.

As Gruff explains today: 'They were formed around two brothers whose parents had moved out: they were left to raise themselves at a very early age! And the house turned into a 24-hour jam session. They became incredible musicians and a magnet to loads of other kids.'

Dafydd's management of the local pop sensation wasn't the only thing he had going for him: one day he had the idea of staging an outdoor music event in the heart of town. The Pesda Roc festival would take place on the site – now a rugby pitch – where, in the thirteenth century, Prince Dafydd had trained his troops to prepare for battle against the Normans. It was a mischievous, genius idea – and battle was indeed about to commence.

Traditionally there weren't many rock 'n' roll freaks in Bethesda; the working-class quarry town had been mostly insulated from the punk craze while developing its own modest subcultures. However, when Pesda Roc kicked off it brought the whole zoo to town, with the high street suddenly crawling with greasy aliens, biker gangs and proto-ravers.

On the first night of the festival, Maffia Mr Huws were headlining the main stage while Gruff and his best mate Rhodri decided to hang back with a few beers. Suddenly from the shadows, a gang of outsiders approached – led by a teenager with a peroxide mohawk.

'Good evening!' came the charming burr. 'I'm Rhys Ifans and

these are my cronies. We were just handing out free copies of my fanzine *Poen Mefwl*[2] – and were wondering if you'd care for a copy?'

'Thankyou!' said Rhodri, taking one.

The Mohawk took a suspicious look around the park, chewing on his cocktail stick. 'Not a bad festival you have here,' he mused. 'Although I must say the locals haven't exactly held us to their bosoms. One person even attempted to beat the shit out of me . . .'

'Ah, sorry to hear that,' said Gruff.

'Not a problem. To be honest, it was probably my own fault. I shook him by the balls, you see.'

Gruff and Rhodri nodded slowly.

'Right, we'd best be off. If you see a man with a spade coming this way, please pass on my sincerest regrets.'

He let out a howling laugh, and scuttled away with the gang.

'What a charismatic man,' said Rhodri. 'Who the fuck is he?'

'I don't really know,' said Gruff, 'but my sister calls him "the wildest man in North Wales". People talk about him as if he's some sort of folk legend.'

'The wildest man in North Wales? Christ, he must be mental.' Rhodri collapsed against a tree. 'So what was it you were talking about a minute ago – about the songs you wrote?'

'Ah, yeah,' said Gruff. 'Basically the walk to school is ridiculously boring, so I've started coming up with a few melodies in my head, and working them out on my brother's guitar.'

'Hang on, though,' said Rhodri. 'Your brother's guitar is left-handed, isn't it?'

'Yeah.'

'And you're right-handed?'

'Yeah, but I've learned to play right-handed on the left-handed.'

Rhodri blinked, then went eyeball to eyeball with his friend.

2 'The Pain of Thought'

He explained how it was time to form a band, how the pop world was opening up, and how together they could mess with people's heads. In the distance, they could hear Maffia Mr Huws drawing the cheers of a thousand people in the night. It was time to form a pop group.

The cards fell easily enough, with Gruff becoming the band's vocalist, and Rhodri finding his place on guitar. The next job was to find more members, and first to volunteer was a local teenage prankster called Andrew Roberts. Andrew was a heavy metal fanatic with a reputation for insane publicity stunts – a reputation that was about to prove particularly useful.

On the day of their first school gig, disaster had apparently struck: the first band had pulled out, threatening to render the whole concert redundant. Andrew had an idea, though, and volunteered to open as a solo act. An hour later, he strode on stage in a spandex jumpsuit and performed a virtuoso heavy metal guitar solo.

'The audience's jaws dropped,' says Gruff today. 'He was on his knees giving it everything.'

So hypnotised were the crowd, in fact, that they didn't notice a discreet wire connecting his amplifier to a cassette recorder. 'He'd tape-recorded obscure heavy metal solos from his record collection,' explains Gruff, 'then fed them into the amp. I think he was miming to Gary Moore solos.'

Backstage, Gruff and Rhodri were getting butterflies. It was ten minutes until stage time, and to compound matters, Gruff still hadn't decided whether he was a left-handed guitarist or a right-handed one. Panicking at the eleventh hour, he suggested a different route altogether.

'You want to play an electric drill?' said Rhodri.

Gruff showed Rhodri the drill.

'Jesus,' said Rhodri, studying the power tool. 'OK. Tell you what, I'll play the guitar and you sit next to me, drilling into my instrument – like this.' Rhodri demonstrated the act. 'But wait,' he suddenly added. 'What about the safety implications?'

'Well,' said Gruff, 'if I drill my guts out and die on stage, at least it'll be entertaining.'

After a few weeks they decided on a name: Ffa Coffi Pawb. It was especially endearing to Rhodri and Gruff because, when pronounced fast enough, it bears a passing resemblance to 'Fuck Off Everybody' – although its literal meaning is the more family-friendly 'Everybody's Coffee Beans'.

Inspired by New Order, the Velvets and Welsh-language post-punk, Ffa Coffi Pawb began to make crude recordings with a drum machine. In their heads they were John Cale and Lou Reed, learning how to piece songs together for the first time. It wasn't long before a cassette had been created, which they proudly called *Torrwyr Beddau Byd-Eang Cyf*,[3] and attempted to sell at the local pub. Their sales pitch was simple: they would dare people to listen.

'You'll regret buying this,' Rhodri warned a local farmer. 'The quality is terrible! The music is offensive!'

The farmer, charmed by this ironic self-deprecation, bought the tape and returned home only to discover the horrible truth: that the music, patched together on a ZX Spectrum, was indeed terrible.

Ffa Coffi Pawb didn't immediately make waves, but their rock 'n' roll reputation was secure when they were almost busted, at a gig in Bangor. 'Andrew was miming, I was drilling and a saxophone player was playing free jazz over the top,' remembers Gruff of the concert, 'and somehow the police got involved because some kids

---

[3] 'Grave Diggers International Ltd'

had broken into the canteen tills while we were playing. Our reputation was tarnished because we had apparently inspired an act of lunacy.'

Their fortunes were about to turn around. A local punk rocker called Rhys Mwyn was getting pissed off that nobody was getting off their arses to create the music scene. He'd already founded a band, Anhrefn, which everybody loved. He'd then started a label, Anhrefn Records, which everybody also loved. The only confusing thing was that nobody loved it enough to try it out themselves. 'Don't they know how easy it is to set up a cassette label?' he thought.

Devising a plan to empower the masses, Mwyn put up posters calling for the most creative musical minds in the area to meet on a weekly basis, so they could swap philosophies, create labels, and make the scene.

Anhrefn were one of the most inspirational groups around – proactive, subversive, almost Dadaist in their sense of humour. What's more, they offered an alternative to what could sometimes seem like counter-productively negative politics.

'A lot of Welsh culture was defined by being anti-English in the 1970s,' says Gruff today. 'We're talking about countries that were once at war, so the atrocities were endless, and the conditions that the Welsh people were expected to live in for centuries after those wars were horrendous. But that's not an excuse to feel animosity for the English people or the English language – it's about finding the positives in yourself and getting on with your neighbours. People are tied by blood, family, habits, collective TV viewing . . . and punk bands like Anhrefn were challenging people to be proud of their own identities without disparaging other people's right to have one.'

When Gruff saw the posters, for him it was a no-brainer to attend Mwyn's meetings. The discussion group became known as

Pop Positif, and it was here that Gruff and Rhodri were to meet the George Martin of their careers – a man whose production skills would tower over the coming decade of Welsh indie coolness. Gorwel Owen was ten years older than Ffa Coffi Pawb, and considerably more musically advanced. He'd dabbled with house music since 1983, and had a reputation as a maverick producer.

At the meeting, Gorwel flipped Gruff and Rhodri a pound for their cassette, and phoned them back the next day. 'Come to my studio tomorrow at noon. Bring your guitars.'

Gorwel was on a whole new level. For a start, he knew how to work drum machines – which in the age of New Order appeared to be the future of rock and roll. However, he was also a focused man with a no-nonsense attitude. 'He made sure we didn't perceive the studio as an extension of our social life,' says Gruff of his first experience with the producer. 'It was very studious. For a while we were scared to swear in front of him – we didn't want to disrespect him, but he was very encouraging.'

For his part, Gorwel was aware that he'd met a sharp bunch of minds. 'It's quite rare for a group to be both exceptional songwriters and to have a really open approach to experimenting with recording,' he says now.

Their first recordings were broadcast almost immediately as a session on BBC Radio Cymru. This wasn't quite as momentous an achievement as it might sound: at the time, anyone who'd recorded a decent-quality Welsh-language demo could reasonably expect to have it broadcast, thanks to the variety of media set up to keep the language flowing (and the relatively few bands that were taking advantage of it).

During the summer of 1988, Ffa Coffi Pawb evolved into the line-up that was to last the rest of its lifetime. There was Rhodri Puw on guitar, Dewi Emlyn on bass, Gruff singing and Dafydd Ieuan on drums: Gruff had stayed in touch with Daf since their time sharing drum classes at the youth club. After being reunited, the two became musical allies and moved in together.

> **FURRY FILE: DAF**
>
> BORN – Bangor, 1969
> CHILDHOOD SUPERPOWER – Flying, swimming
> CHILDHOOD SUPERWEAKNESS – Not being able to fly or swim
> CLASSROOM DISASTER – 'Sneaking off to school at five years old in my paisley pyjamas, 'cos I thought I looked like Gary Glitter'
> CHILDHOOD VICTORY – 'Realising that a man-made, invisible, supernatural, totalitarian being, that demanded to be praised lest it condemn you to eternal torture in hell, was a bag of shite'
> TEEN REBEL ICON – Ffred Ffrancis, Welsh Language Activist
> TEEN GROOMING TIP – Tooth brushing
> GEEKY PASSION: Pigs ('I wanted to breed them and make money')
> FIRST SONGWRITING ATTEMPT – 'Llanaelhaearn Lleddf (Blues)',1979
> BEACH BOYS VALHALLA – 'Till I Die'
> LIFE WISDOM: 'Don't be a cunt' – Jim Jeffries

As the eighties gave way to the nineties, Ffa Coffi Pawb's songwriting continued to blossom: Rhodri was inspired by the early work of Happy Mondays and the Stone Roses, while Gruff and Daf began thinking about the craft of pop music, reasoning that every great tune should kick off with a memorable hook.

Gorwel remembers a philosophy that they adopted at this time:

'I recall them saying that "the studio is just a vehicle for the songs". That's very true, of course, but they also understood that the opposite was true: that songs can be vehicles for experimenting.'

The experimenting was paying off too: for one matter, Gruff finally resolved the dilemma of which way round to play the guitar. Trained left-handed, but in possession of only a right, he simply flipped the guitar upside-down.

As 1991 dawned, the runway for Ffa Coffi Pawb was clear for take-off. Not only had they settled on a 'fab four' line-up and started writing great songs, but they had an occasional harmonica player too: the Wildest Man in North Wales. From the beginning, Rhys Ifans had a strong belief that he was going to be a professional actor; but of all the musicians he dabbled with, he was undoubtedly the most rock 'n' roll.

One winter's afternoon, the band had just finished sound-checking at a small club in Porthmadog when Rhys and Rhodri went outside to see what the crowds were like.

'Crikey,' said Rhodri. 'The only thing missing is tumbleweed. I guess we'll be playing to the sound engineer again.'

'There, there, Rhodri,' said Rhys, slurping a cocktail with a twinkle in his eye. 'It just so happens that I know precisely where to get a massive crowd from. You go back inside and set up with the band, and I'll be back in five minutes with an audience.'

'Five minutes?'

'Five minutes,' winked Rhys.

He jogged down the street to a crossroads, then stopped and looked around, smelling the wind for signs of life. Suddenly a cheer resonated from a bar called The Headless Ram. Rhys swung through the door and coughed loudly.

'Good afternoon, ladies!' he said, silencing a roomful of leather-bound men. He cleared his throat and started again.

'Word has it . . . that there is a rather good biker rock band playing just round the corner at the club tonight. The *best* biker band in North Wales, in fact!'

The bikers stared at him. One of them folded his arms.

'And apparently it's free beer too. I'll be going now.' He grinned and slowly began to crab-walk out again.

That night, Ffa Coffi Pawb performed their pop music to a gang of confused, hairy men. As the final notes rang out to reveal an eerie silence, it became apparent that some sort of reconciliatory gesture was required. Rhys stepped up to the microphone. 'Would anybody like to buy a tape?'

# CHAPTER 3

## ANKST RECORDS /
## GORKY'S ZYGOTIC MYNCI /
## WHY AREN'T WE MAKING TECHNO? /
## THE LONG WALK HOME

'It's ten past three in the morning, this is Radio Cymru and *that* was Ffa Coffi Pawb! Now we've got something a little bit different for you, a new band from Pembrokeshire. They're only fifteen years old and this is their first ever session. One word of warning, though: I've got a sneaky feeling the lyrics to this one are in English . . . do you think we can get away with it? Put it this way: it's the middle of the night, so if you don't tell the BBC, I won't. Let's have it for Gorky's Zygotic Mynci.'

Before 1991, Welsh bands had relatively few choices regarding who to sign with. The biggest contender was the major label Sain, which had put out some decent folk albums in the 1970s but was by now deemed deeply uncool. As Gruff explains, 'They'd got into Aled Jones and choirs, sheep farmers singing Elvis songs in Welsh . . . they were like a dinosaur back then.' At the other end of the spectrum was Rhys Mwyn's punk label Anhrefn: it was established and hip – but also radical, niche and somewhat limited in reach. There was clearly a gap for a label that could sit between the goalposts; and that label was Ankst.

Ankst Records was set up as an independent operation by Alun Llwyd, Gruffudd Jones and Emyr Glyn Williams while they were students at Aberystwyth University. The three of them were music fans rather than musicians themselves – indeed, they had no *desire* to become musicians – and therefore they were free to stay in the background and concentrate on nurturing artists.

'Ankst were absolutely crucial,' says Gorwel Owen today. 'They created a space for the creative process to happen, which is one of the most important things that a label can do.'

The founders of Ankst quickly established it as a launch pad for the new generation of Welsh pop, folk and hip hop – and, being massive fans of Ffa Coffi Pawb – soon approached them with a record deal for two EPs.

'Gruff is one of those natural musicians – he's never going to stop writing pop songs,' says the label's co-founder Emyr Glyn Williams. 'Even back then the songs were catchy, clever, psychedelic and musically ambitious. He wanted to make great albums, as he still does now. So for us it was a safe bet to help them, and work with them. They were one of the best bands around at the time, and we were big fans.'

Although Ankst had initially run a Welsh-language-only policy, the emergence of bilingual bands such as Gorky's Zygotic Mynci had prompted them to reconsider. 'I think it was the bands that changed Ankst,' says Emyr. 'We responded to the circumstances, particularly with Gorky's because they were bilingual from the beginning, and quite naturally so.'

Ankst were super-enthusiastic about Gorky's, a band of teenagers from Carmarthen, South Wales, with massive potential. Getting them played on Radio Cymru was another matter, however: it was left to rebellious, late-night DJs like Nia Melville to play them. 'She had great taste,' says Gruff. 'It wasn't anything to do with language, it was just whether she liked the music or not. Radio Cymru scrapped the show after a year because they thought it was too weird – they couldn't see how pioneering it was.'

Oblivious to the arguments happening around them, Gorky's mixture of folk, psychedelic Dadaism and Fall-inspired rock immediately clicked with a young audience both in Wales and England, and suddenly the *NME* and John Peel counted themselves among the band's supporters. This was something new.

'The *NME* had looked to Wales on and off before this,' says Emyr. 'It would usually be an overview with a few bands, but then those bands would never really have careers – they'd never be able to make the albums and keep going. And the interest would be "We've done our article on Welsh bands now" – and that would be it.

'With Gorky's [the music press] saw what we saw: they were a young, extraordinary band – and I think some of the journalists fell for them, like they became their favourite band. The Welsh thing never got in the way for them, because Gorky's weren't stridently political like other Welsh bands, they were quite different.'

While Gorky's were attracting the attention of the London music papers, Ffa Coffi Pawb had arrived at the end of the road. Over the course of two albums with Ankst their sound had evolved into blissful, reverb-drenched bubblegum pop, owing as much to The Jesus and Mary Chain as to Big Star. However, where this melodic direction had once felt fresh against the backdrop of avant-garde and punk bands, the band eventually came to suspect that they'd become too conventional – and were letting audience expectations lead the way.

Rhodri attempted to head off this suspicion by rebelling against melody: under the influence of dark industrial bands like Nitzer Ebb, he began playing sets full of gnashing distortion and droning single notes.

This was a new lease of life for the guitarist, but it wouldn't be long before a more literal lease of life – the arrival of his first baby – would distract him from the band. Increasingly, Gruff and

Daf were beginning to find themselves alone in the studio to cover what instruments they could. The band's convictions took a further knock every time they heard the weird electronic music coming off Gorwel Owen's stereo: surreal, progressive music with samples and twisted beats. By these standards, the band that Gruff and Rhodri had started five years previously sounded suspiciously traditional.

Ffa Coffi Pawb played their final gig at the Builth Wells Eisteddfod in 1993, with Gorky's supporting and just over a thousand people in attendance.

In the sleeve notes to their final album, *Hei Vidal!*, they addressed the conundrum they faced directly – but also hinted at the future: 'I mean for f'sakes it's 1992, and what are we? Mods, rockers, post-mod rockers? Why aren't we making techno records?!'

# CHAPTER 4

**THE TEACHER /
ROCK AND SQUAT /
CARDIFF IN THE SUN / THE RAVE**

Later that summer, Gruff was sitting on the roof of a train – speeding briskly through the luminous green forests of Mid Wales. Sitting up alongside him was a teacher he'd met at the party below – a party which they both agreed was crap.

The plan had been simple: Gruff would assist a band of hedonists in transporting a crate of booze between Llanuwchllyn and Bala, after which he could either crash at the party or split with his share of the crate. Something had gone wrong, however: the hedonists had drunk the booze on the train, and subsequently gone out of their minds. Gruff and the teacher – who was equally embroiled and equally confused – had no option but to sneak politely out of the window.

Still, the roof of the train was a serene place to be, and while the teacher explained that he, too, played in a band, Gruff experimented with lifting a beer up to his face, using the force of the wind to surf it towards his mouth.

Suddenly, however, the train began to puff to a crawl. Gruff raised an eyebrow at the teacher.

'Let's get down!'

They sky-dived back through the window, kicked the cans

under the seats and neatened their shaggy hair. Seconds later, the guard came in and slammed the door behind him.

'Right, lads,' he said with vaguely sadistic enthusiasm. 'Who's been sitting on my train then?'

After a few seconds' pause for thought, a hand lifted up from behind a seat, and pointed at Gruff. Then another hand appeared, pointing at the teacher. The two accused could not quite believe what was happening: this was not *Spartacus*. This was the opposite of *Spartacus*.

'Right! You two, out!'

Gruff and the teacher stood in the middle of the tracks as the train pulled away, slowly coming to terms with their new environment. The situation didn't look promising: the horizon stretched for miles with field and forest, the sun was fading, and to make matters worse a crow was hopping about in front of them.

'We're fucked,' concluded the teacher. 'That crow is definitely a sign that we're fucked.' The two of them estimated that it was an hour's walk to Bala, although they could probably hitch their way in half that time. The road was deserted and the sun was setting. They began to walk.

'And that's how I really got to know Gruff,' says Bunf today. 'It was interesting that it was him and me, for almost no apparent reason, meeting like that. You couldn't have made it up.'

## FURRY FILE: BUNF

BORN – Cardiff, 1967
CHILDHOOD SUPERPOWER – 'My Puma football boots'
CHILDHOOD SUPERWEAKNESS – Sweetcorn
CHILDHOOD DISASTER – Burning down parents' living room

> CHILDHOOD VICTORY – Winning a womble in a raffle ('I believe it was Great Uncle Bulgaria')
> BAD BEHAVIOUR – Perennial daydreaming
> TEEN REBEL ICON – Gianluca Vialli, Juventus and Italian striker ('He had a sneaky cigarette while he was a sub during the World Cup ... the commentator Barry Davies didn't know what to say')
> TEEN GROOMING TIP – Leather jacket
> GEEKY PASSION – Sharks
> FIRST ATTEMPTED SONG – 'Swn' ('It means noise ... I had no idea what I was doing')
> BEACH BOYS VALHALLA – 'Good Vibrations'
> LIFE WISDOM – 'Never judge a book by its cover'

Bunf was the guitarist in a band called U Thant. All the posters said that U Thant were a punk band, but somewhere along the road they'd taken a left turn into space-rock territory, and now Bunf was armed to the teeth with psychedelic guitar pedals.

Totally uninterested in learning the blues, playing hyperspeed solos or even being technically any good, Bunf was instead on a mission to find his own sound. Three heroes, at the time, were pointing the way.

'Tone-wise it was Mick Ronson,' he says of the legendary glam-rock guitarist. 'In terms of stage presence it was Chuck Berry, and [I wanted] the pacing of George Harrison's solos. To be honest, I never did crack Chuck Berry.'

When he wasn't being a psychedelic rock star, Bunf worked in education – and following two years at a primary school, he'd graduated to being head of art at a secondary near Pontypridd. To the kids, Bunf was a source of dazed amusement, arriving late in the mornings to find that they'd already registered themselves and started without him.

'I managed to get the two most responsible girls to help out,' he says now. 'If I was five minutes late they would take over the register. It's not what you're supposed to do as a teacher, but in a way I think they enjoyed it, because it empowered them to take responsibility . . . in my own sick way I taught them a lesson!'

The other teachers at school, however, viewed Bunf with suspicion – and the feeling was mutual. Organised religion and discipline were the twin forks of the school's philosophy, with the deputy heads in particular displaying an evangelical streak. It wasn't the religion that bothered Bunf, however; more the school's insistence that religion alone could save kids from a life of poverty. 'We were in a really hard, deprived area which had this enormous lack of hope,' says Bunf, 'and it was inadequate to suggest that it'd be OK if you followed that path. The kids were beyond that.'

When possible Gruff and Daf would catch the teacher in action with U Thant, and it wasn't long before they got to know another member of the group who seemed a like-minded kind of person: Guto Pryce, their dark-haired, square-jawed bass player.

---

## FURRY FILE: GUTO

BORN – Cardiff, 1972
CHILDHOOD DISASTER – 'Having to make do with a hand-me-down pink Raleigh Commando bike instead of a BMX'
CHILDHOOD VICTORY – 'Bunnyhopping that Commando'
BAD BEHAVIOUR – Cross-country running fraud
TEEN REBEL ICON – Diego Maradona
TEEN GROOMING TIP – Dungarees
GEEK SPECIALITY – *Oink!* comic

> FIRST SONGWRITING ATTEMPT – 'Mynd Am Dro', 1978 ('It was basically a rip-off of a Welsh song about two dogs that go for a walk in the woods and lose a shoe')
> BEACH BOYS VALHALLA – 'Big Sur'
> LIFE WISDOM – 'Bunf once told me: "Don't eat anything bigger than your head"'

Guto had grown up on a diet of punk and melodic pop, supplied to him respectively by The Damned and ELO. His earliest encounter with the bass guitar was watching the French TV superstar Jean-Jacques Burnel, who not only played bass, but also knew karate; very cool indeed.

Like Gruff, Guto's adventures in rock and roll started early. 'It's funny,' he says today, 'I don't think you can do it now, but back then you could start a band and easily get on TV, then pick up a cheque for £140 at the end of the day. So you'd form bands just to get on telly, earn a bit of money.'

After a couple of years playing Ramones covers in a garage band, Guto signed up for U Thant. For some time the group enjoyed playing the 'rock 'n' squat' scenes of Eastern Europe, and at just seventeen years old found themselves playing in the former East Germany. 'It was quite nuts really,' says Guto, 'and an eye-opener when you're seventeen. We were playing to a bunch of Iron Maiden fans every night, classic punk rockers – they'd seen Camden Town on a postcard and thought "I want to be zis!"'

At the dawn of 1991, U Thant were comfortably nestled in their home town of Cardiff. However, before their counterparts in Ffa Coffi Pawb could join them, a brief geographical diversion was about to occur: Manchester.

Gruff and Daf moved to the city of dance music together, in an attempt to kick-start their art educations at the university. To their delight, the acid house scene was in full bloom – and for a few months they embarked on a hedonistic holiday in the 'second summer of love', checking out the 24-hour nightclubs and casually noting the latest techno sounds.

Yet Daf soon became contemplative and, disillusioned with art education and spooked by the suspicion that he was neglecting his one true calling, music, he decided to move back to Cardiff. Although the move separated him from his best friend, it was a pivotal decision: the flat he was moving into would shortly become the arts lab of the Super Furry Animals.

Daf unpacked his bags on the wooden floors of 12 Column Road, Cardiff on 5 June 1993. Moving in alongside him were his girlfriend Debbie, Rhys Ifans, and Rhys's strange Polish girlfriend who enjoyed shoplifting. Before they could get round to settling in, however, the phone rang. It was Bunf.

'We were thinking about taking some acid, and then going to watch the dinosaurs at the museum,' he said. 'Would you like to come along?'

Daf put the phone down and smiled at his girlfriend. 'Fucking 'ell, I think I like this guy!'

That night, the acid was far too strong, forcing them to walk very slowly and carefully back to Bunf's flat, under the watchful eye of strange lights emanating from the traffic. Inside, Daf switched on the living-room light to reveal a labyrinthine city of guitar-effects pedals on the floor. They had entered Bunf's space-rock HQ.

'Pedals,' whispered Daf, pointing at the floor, the wall, then the ceiling too. 'Pedals,' he repeated. 'Everywhere!'

It was Cardiff's hottest summer for twenty years, and the surf was definitely up: living in the capital, Daf got to sample the countryside raves that were exploding in its satellite countryside. There was also an additional benefit to living in the city: he got to hang out with his younger brother, Cian – a film student living up the road in Newport.

## FURRY FILE: CIAN

BORN – Bangor, 1976
SUPERPOWER – Flight
SUPERWEAKNESS – Sleep deprivation
CHILDHOOD DISASTER – 'I was caught with my trousers around my ankles in primary school, when the fire alarm went off. I had to go on yard in my pants and all had a good laugh at my expense'
CHILDHOOD VICTORY – 'Winning the Albert Owen shield with Pentraeth FC'
BAD BEHAVIOUR – 'I never got caught!'
REBEL ICON – Diego Maradona
TEENAGE GROOMING TIP – Eyeliner
GEEK DISCLOSURE – Lego
FIRST ATTEMPTED SONG – 'I remember recording myself doing raspberries into the tape machine when I was about six years old'
BEACH BOYS VALHALLA – 'Forever'

Cian was too young to go raving, but he was nonetheless an acid house fan. One track that proved particularly influential to the young teenager was the Snowman mix of 'Humanoid' – in part a rave version of *The Snowman* soundtrack – by an early incarnation of The Future Sound of London.

With Orbital also making regular appearances on the turntables, it was only a matter of time until Cian started to make his own dance music, making his earliest recordings onto DAT tapes. As Cian explains today, it was a time of experimentation and creation.

'I had this teacher who'd say something like "Ideas are a penny apiece, it's how you execute them that makes them special." Which was frustrating at the time because I thought all my ideas were worth something, and it seemed like he brought you right down: anyone can have an idea! But it influenced me from that point on, not to get hung up on an idea – the next one would always be better, and if you get a good one and execute it well . . . that's where the magic is.'

By the time Cian had started to apply this magic to samplers and synths, his older brother was going out and dancing to them. One night in June 1994, Bunf, Guto, Rhys, Daf and Gruff – who was down from Manchester for the weekend – partied at Cardiff's Hippo Club until 2am, then jumped into Bunf's Ford Fiesta and set the coordinates for the heart of a rave. In those pre-satnav times, their journey into the countryside was a challenge in itself: first they drove out to the outskirts of Merthyr, then they sped up the dual carriageway before finally pulling up in a floodlit Asda car park, along with thirty or so mysterious vehicles.

Daf wound down the window and spotted a tall, dreadlocked man shouting at the cars like some kind of crazed traffic controller.

'That's him, *that's* the man,' he said. 'He's the one telling people how to get there. HEY! YOU! WHERE ARE WE HEADING?'

'South exit, follow the convoy!' shouted the dreadlocks, prompting Bunf to rev up the engine and fall in line.

Several miles later, they were zooming through a wide stretch of moonlit countryside, spiralling in and out of the cover of forest.

There was just one problem: it was becoming increasingly difficult to tell which cars to follow: the trail of ravers was running cold, diluted with regular traffic. Stuck for a solution, the car pulled over and Gruff got out to have a listen. At first, there was only open sky, cricket chirps and wind. But then:

OOM OOM OOM
OOM OOM OOM
OOM OOM OOM

The sound of muffled drums rolled towards them, then rolled back again. 'Festival wind!' thought Gruff. Rhys came out to offer a second opinion, and they both stood there a while, surveying the ambience. 'It appears to be coming from the direction of the trees!' announced Rhys in a Shakespearean accent.

A debate ensued as to what the blazes to do next. Then a police car sped past.

'Follow the cops!'

Unaware of their secret tail, the police descended downhill then turned into an incongruous lane – thick on each side with overgrown grass. Bunf slowly turned off to follow them, separated by a short distance, and the two cars trundled along uneven ground for five minutes. Finally, a sense of nervous excitement emerged as garden candles began to appear, lighting up the route and guiding them along. The darkness became pierced by the glare of distant torches beyond the trees, and the OOM OOM OOM grew louder.

'Time to leave our friends behind,' said Bunf, turning off and rolling carefully into a shallow ditch. And that was that. They got out, and a few of them lit roll-ups with mischievous grins on their faces.

'Who the fuck are all these people?' cooed Daf, gazing up at the shadowy figures walking past, silhouetted on the hill. Just then, a girl in fluorescent angel wings and a fluffy bra ran past, shouting ahead to her friends.

'Jesus,' laughed Rhys, exhaling smoke out of his nostrils. 'It's a super furry animal!'

Three hours later, Gruff and Daf were lying down next to a makeshift campfire while the others were off dancing. They looked out across the rave, spread over the hill before them. A helter-skelter had been built on the horizon, from which DJs were firing out echoed beats that cracked like fireworks in the night. In the middle of the carnival, they spotted Euros Childs, the singer of Gorky's Zygotic Mynci, walking past. Euros saw them and began shouting something undecipherable.

'WHAT?!?' shouted Gruff.

'LISTEN TO *SURF'S UP*!' yelled Euros, who laughed and carried on walking.

'Does he mean the Beach Boys album?' asked Daf. 'Why the fuck did he say that?'

'Ah, we're just having an ongoing conversation about the Beach Boys, advising each other on what to investigate.'

Daf stroked his jaw and paused for thought. 'Which Beach Boy was it that had that massive beard?'

'I think they all had pretty good beards for a while . . . Dennis had a fantastic beard. Mike Love had a beard for the majority of the Beach Boys' career, I think. When he started losing his hair, the beard came.'

'The beard came?'

'It grew in inverse proportion to the hair loss. It was a strange kind of correlation.'

Daf laughed, then pointed to the campfire. 'Jesus, your boots are on fire!'

After dousing his feet in beer, they sat back to watch the festivities again. Time was ticking on: in two months Gruff would graduate from Manchester and join his friends in Cardiff. Naturally there was talk of a new band. The idea was a loose one: it would be electronic, lucid, a forward-looking collective with a shape-shifting line-up. They could combine different languages, mix disparate musical forms, take their imaginations for a ride.

'It's a tough cookie,' said Daf, 'but we can't play the minority-language circuit for ever. It's time we started *really* communicating – as in, communicating with the whole fucking world!'

Gruff laughed and turned to look back at the skyline. U Thant had just broken up, leaving Bunf and Guto free to form an alliance. The DJ beats cracked and echoed towards him, illuminated by a glowing valley of sparks.

'You're right,' he finally said. 'Let's get our shit together.'

# CHAPTER 5
## SFA SOUNDSYSTEM /
## THE MAN DON'T GIVE A DUB /
## RHYS SAYS ADIOS / INTO SPACE

The SFA Soundsystem was designed for maximum flexibility. With a battered mixing desk, three synths, one sequencer and an acid-rock guitarist among its arsenal, on the one hand it was a techno beast, on the other a space-rock cruiser.

Most impressively, it was also mobile. Most of the techno gear was stored in a box that could easily be driven to a local party, no band required. The SFA rep would simply push the button, punch in the variables, and let the Soundsystem off its leash. This flexibility meant that over the next year Guto, Daf and Gruff played as a techno trio in Brittany; Bunf and Cian played as a dub duo in Pontyberry; and Rhys sang over a space-rock quintet in Cardiff. Membership of SFA Soundsystem was as fluid as its music, lending the era a sense of loose, heady magic.

The collective's mischievous philosophy was cemented when they played a short tour with the Welsh post-punk group Anhrefn: a band who insisted on challenging and confounding their audiences rather than appeasing them; a band who delivered political discourse and radicalism with almost Dadaist humour.

'We're going to be as big as Guns N' Roses!' screamed Rhys one night, having just grilled a folk festival with a setlist of dub techno. For all the fun they were having, however, there were still danger signs: in particular, they were wary of the 'rave rock' tag and its cheesy implications. To see this off, they endeavoured to only incorporate the elements of dance music that they really liked, building something melodic, new and personal around them.

An evolutionary gear-change occurred one night when the band returned to Daf's flat from an outdoor rave, and decided to come down to the Beach Boys album *Surf's Up*. After a few minutes' listening to the album that Euros Childs had recommended, they suddenly made a connection. As Guto explains: 'That's when we realised that, "fuckin 'ell, *Surf's Up* features some really cool synths like that rave record – it's almost the same sound!" We'd see the connection there, and it was basically Moog synthesisers.'

That summer was to be a time of innovative electronica, big beats and blissful surf harmonies – three elements that would swim together in the band's eventual DNA – and with Rhys Ifans on vocals, they set to work.

The Super Furry Animals' first major achievement would spring directly from their dance music roots, and specifically the form's hypnotic, unapologetic sense of repetition.

In its earliest form, 'The Man Don't Give a Fuck' was a dub exercise, whipped together during a day-long improvisation at Daf's parents' house.

The drummer had sampled the lyric '*You know they don't give a fuck about anybody else*' from the Steely Dan track 'Showbiz Kids', and invited the band to play over the top. As the loop kicked into life, the musicians couldn't help but burst out laughing: it was at once ludicrously catchy and perfectly anti-establishment. They'd never heard anything like it, and yet it contained elements of everything they were into.

The dub version of 'The Man Don't Give a Fuck' prompted

the band to lay down their first recording, and on the tail end of a 48-hour party in Manchester, they cut across North Wales to record it at Gorwel Owen's Anglesey studio, alongside a song called 'Of No Fixed Identity'. The session connected the band with the man who would eventually become their mentor and producer, although the results remain unreleased to this day.

When Gruff finally touched down in Cardiff, the city was facing an epic season of torrential rain. What's more, the weather wasn't the only thing keeping people indoors: the free party scene had been gathering momentum over the previous year, with soundsystems like Spiral Tribe and DIY entertaining crowds of up to 20,000 people at spontaneous outdoor festivals. There was just one problem: they were being watched. After observing with a twitchy eye for some months, the British government finally clamped down on the raves with brutal efficiency. The 1994 Criminal Justice Act made it illegal to hold outdoor parties consisting of more than 100 people. The bill also gave the police a licence to arrest two people or more if they appeared to even be *waiting* for a rave, and it reserved particular venom for any music that resembled a 'succession of repetitive beats'. Within weeks the Cardiff party scene was transformed, and with little alternative, the era of outdoor raves mutated into club-land. Things hadn't become boring exactly, but they had certainly become restricted.

In July 1993, SFA continued to record new demos, though it soon became apparent that something wasn't quite in sync. Rhys's habit of snoozing unconsciously after a few ales meant he kept curling up into a ball on the floor of the recording studio, often while the red light was on. Then another Rhys-related problem came along: it emerged that he was being offered high-profile acting jobs – and, worse, turning them down out of his sense of loyalty to the band. When they discovered this, the other Furries were concerned. To them it was inconceivable that Rhys wouldn't take the ticket and pursue his love for acting; if anything, it would be a tragic missed opportunity for him. In a different lifetime Rhys might have ended up singing for the Super Furry Animals – but it was not to be this one. After an affectionate chat, they parted ways with the Wildest Man in North Wales – but it would be far from the last of their adventures together.

After a month of torrential rain, things finally started looking up. Firstly, Daf received a letter from Nia Melville at Radio Cymru, offering the band a live session. Ecstatic for the first time in months, the Furries threw their support behind Gruff becoming the new singer of the band, and – after some initial hesitation about returning to centre stage – he agreed.

Two songs were recorded quickly and with inspired results. The first, 'Dim Brys Dim Chwys', remains one of the most dance-inspired tracks SFA have ever produced: hinging on hypnotic breakbeats and an ever-ascending feeling of space euphoria, it has the telling feel of an outdoor soundsystem in action. Meanwhile, the second song, 'Blerwytirhwng?', would be the bait that secured the Super Furries' first record deal.

Ankst Records were riding a wave at the time, with Gorky's scoring a number one in the independent album charts, and Catatonia attracting the likes of the *NME* and Radio One. The label hadn't forgotten Gruff and Daf's fuzzy pop songs with Ffa Coffi Pawb, however, and when they heard about the Furry project, the hottest label in Wales came calling again. After discovering that Gruff had written over forty new songs, Ankst suggested they put out 'Blerwytirhwng?' and record a few extra songs to make up an EP. Yet again, it was time to go back to Gorwel's.

'We were incredibly lucky that we had people like Gorwel, and Les Morrison, who ran a studio in Bethesda,' says Ankst's Emyr. 'To have a recording industry in Wales you've got to have studios

– there's no other way around it. So these people were crucial, and thanks to them a lot of music got released.'

The Furries' move away from dance music was not an overnight one: even while they had toured Brittany as a techno band, Gruff and Daf had been working on more conventional songs. Pop music had long been part of their DNA, and with an EP to record they instinctively leaned in its direction.

Amused by the defiantly ridiculous name of a village in North Wales, the Furries named their debut EP *Llanfairpwllgwngyllgogerychwyndrobwllantysiliogogogochynygofod* – although perhaps as a concession to those who couldn't pronounce it, *In Space* was also offered as a subtitle.

In some ways, the record is the sound of Daf and Gruff coughing the last few sparks of Ffa Coffi Pawb out of their systems – 'Organ Yn Dy Geg' and 'Crys Ti' have a distinctly Pawb flavour. However, with the casually ambitious pop strut of 'Fix Idris' the Super Furries do announce themselves; it's a song that tunnels through catchy, ascending melodies and broken-robot noise, describing a lifestyle spent 'swimming through space' and watching Tarantino videos.

Throughout the year Daf's catchphrase had been 'We'll be signed by Christmas!' but in reality the band's expectations were more grounded: in the seven years that Ffa Coffi Pawb had been together, they'd played London just once, while Radio One and MTV might as well have existed on a different planet. And yet unbeknown to the Furries, an interstellar alignment was about to take place.

# CHAPTER 6

**BIRTH OF A RINGTONE /
LONDON TURNS ON / MOOG DROOG /
THE WISDOM OF ROBERT PLANT /
OUTLAW AIRCRAFT CARRIER**

Twenty thousand miles above Mexico, the satellite waited. For three months now it had been floating in the orbit of Earth, a white dot against a glowing colossus, not really knowing what the heck it was doing there. Just as it was becoming accustomed to the lullaby of space, however, something beeped.

BE-WOOOW

The satellite opened a bright, orange eye. Suddenly, a row of miniature green lights came on along its starboard side, one after the other, culminating with its dome-shaped head swivelling round and bleeping to attention. It was showtime.

Thousands of miles to the west, another satellite was having the same rude awakening. Despite their distance from one another, they both began swivelling their heads in unison, as if preparing to fire lasers at any moment. They beeped excitedly. Red buttons began flashing. The drums of history beat throughout the galaxy.

Then . . . strangely, nothing. Somebody had apparently cancelled the lasers. Both satellites resumed bobbing gracefully forwards, and went back to sleep. Except one thing had changed inside the second satellite. Within its clean white shell, deep down in the hatch tunnel, there was a dark control room with green lights dancing on a screen. And it was in this room that the silence was crudely broken.

> NEE-NEE-NAW NAW
> NEE-NEE-NAW NAW
> NEE-NEE-NAW NAW-NAW

The Nokia ringtone had breathed its first breath.

Hundreds of miles below, Guto, Gruff, Cian, Bunf and Daf were trundling up a snowy hill towards the Lampeter University student union, where they were scheduled to play their first gig as a rock band. Pausing to take a breath outside the venue, they looked up and saw a poster.

> TONIGHT – SUPER FURY ANIMALS!

'Super *Fury* Animals?' said Daf. 'What the fuck?'

Despite the typo, the gig marked the beginning of a crucial phase for the band. It was at their next show, an Aberystwyth date in March 1995, that they were introduced to Creation Records' A&R man Mark Bowen. Mark shook their hands outside the venue and enthusiastically suggested that the group should come and play London.

The following week, Welsh music journalist Iestyn George was sat at his desk in the *NME* office, chewing gum and contemplating the sound coming from his headphones. He nodded his head, got up and walked purposefully down the aisle of the office, slapping down copies of the *In Space* EP on the desks of other writers.

'They're playing the Water Rats next week,' said George with a sense of excitable duty. 'Let's get down there!'

The Furries' debut show in London would have been virtually empty had it not been for Iestyn's conviction: as it turned out, there were ten music journalists watching the band, and pretty much nobody else.

Wary of coming across as hicks from the sticks, Gruff decided to grab their big city debut by the balls.

'Listen up, motherfuckers!' he yelled, leading SFA into a short, sharp, six-song set. At this stage, the band was a slack live outfit: they had their act together to an extent, but hadn't really taken the time to get tight. Regardless, the writers fell in love – and the following week, Gruff and Daf opened the *NME* to see a full-page live review.

'Fuck me!' blurted Daf, spilling his coffee. 'Does this mean I can come off the dole?'

Back in London, Creation Records' boss Alan McGee was sat at his desk reading the same article. It was his A&R man that had booked the gig, and now that the *NME* was salivating it was clearly time to make a move. McGee decided to do something that was completely out of the ordinary. He decided to go to a rock concert. 'My passion at that time was either women or football,' he says today, 'but I thought that for once I should do my job, so I went to their next show.'

At the Super Furries' next London gig, at the Monarch in Camden Town, it wasn't journalists that made up the audience, it was publishers, record labels, fans – and McGee. 'Nice work, lads,' he said after the show, patting Gruff warmly on the back, 'but you might want to try singing in English next time!' Gruff laughed nervously, keeping it to himself that they had in fact sung in English throughout.

'Right, here's the plan,' said McGee. 'We're gonna put you in the studio. Three days in Fulham to see what we've got. Your man at Ankst tells me there are twenty songs ready to go?'

'Sixty!'

'Fucking great.' After quickly agreeing the schedule, McGee tipped an imaginary hat as he disappeared back into the crowd. 'Play the hits, lads . . . play the hits . . .'

Over the next seven days, Ankst Records were subjected to a flurry of Furry phone enquiries, and with co-founder Alun Llwyd answering the phone every other minute, it was only a matter of time until someone asked the question. 'Are you their manager?'

Alun shrugged his shoulders. 'Yeah, I guess I am!' He put down the phone, unaware that he'd just signed up for a new job.

'Emyr!' he shouted to his Ankst partner. 'You know that limited-edition Furries EP?'

'Yep?'

'Better make it an unlimited edition!'

SFA's final EP for Ankst demonstrated a combination of pop flair and cheeky mischief. The title *Moog Droog* is a knowingly anglicised subversion of the Welsh slang for marijuana ('mwg drwg', meaning 'bad smoke'), as well as a nod to Moog synthesisers and the dystopian 'droogs' in the film *A Clockwork Orange*.

Musically, the EP remains mysterious, fresh and vulnerable to this day. 'Pam V' has an atmosphere of newborn curiosity, building cautiously but inevitably towards an anarchic burst of mischief, while 'God! Show Me Magic' and 'Focus Pocus/Debiel' bring melodic rock action to the table, the latter speeding along like future-punk before suddenly switching to a rainy day sing-along.

Completing the EP, 'Sali Mali' is the one track that would never have an afterlife as a reissue. Named after the Welsh children's literature character whose adventures running a fictional café had taught the band to read, the song is appropriately yearning, gentle and nostalgic.

The Furries were proud of *Moog Droog*, but by the time of its release they were already demo'ing for Creation. While they were multi-tracking a new song called 'Something for the Weekend', McGee appeared in the control room.

'That's a fucking hit, eh?' he said, taking off his sunglasses. 'Right! Here it is: I'm not promising you anything and I'm not saying I'm going to make you all millionaires. But I would like to put your records out. OK? Do we have a deal?'

The Furries assured him they were determined to sell loads of records, and the deal was done. 'I thought I was signing an out-and-out Britpop, Blur kind of band,' McGee says today. 'Little did I know that I was signing The Beach Boys meets Gong meets Isaac Hayes on a fucking acid trip.'

Things kicked off immediately. £20,000 was transferred into the band's bank account, and within forty-eight hours they had spent it all on the most ridiculous, weird-shaped guitars they could find. The guitars sounded terrible, but it didn't matter; they had won the pools, and now was the time for getting on MTV and making ridiculous demands.

The next day the Furries were called to Creation's offices near Primrose Hill for a photo shoot. The label's massive success with Oasis, as well as their deal with Sony (which meant they were effectively backed by the major label) had clearly rubbed off on their interior design: most of Creation was open plan, light and airy.

'It was an open-plan office,' explains Guto today, 'and you'd walk past all these workers saying "Hello! Hello!" You'd usually be a bit drunk too, because of the pub down the road in which you'd have a few beers while waiting to go in. Then you'd go into what felt like the headmaster's office, Dick Green's room.' Green was a co-founder of Creation, and the most hands-on Creation rep when it came to dealing with the band. However, what might have been hands on for other labels was, for Creation, distinctly *hands off*.

'Creation were great, they just let us get on with it,' says Guto. 'We'd been to some record companies and sat in their receptions feeling a bit fucking scruffy. But Creation welcomed us.'

Outside the building, the band were just finishing having their photos taken when a car pulled up and Robert Plant walked out, complete with golden hair and tight trousers. Overhearing the Furries speaking in Welsh, the rock god cheerfully greeted them with a 'Bore da!' and explained in fluent Welsh how he liked to spend time in the valleys. The band tried to keep it cool, presuming that it was an entirely mundane occurrence to bump into international rock stars in London.

'We just signed our first record deal yesterday,' said Guto. 'Do you have any advice?'

'How about this,' offered Plant. 'When you have your photo taken, always look up – it hides your double chin.'

Once they'd shaken hands with Plant, the band met up with Creation's new product manager John Andrews and headed over to the pub. Andrews was an astute and creative man with a smart head on his shoulders, and having started working for Creation at the same time as the Furries, he felt a strong affinity with the band.

That first meeting set the tone for meetings to come: the band got hammered and made ridiculous demands while Andrews shrewdly took notes, staying sober and deciphering the possible from the impossible. The Furries' first demand was that Creation buy them an aircraft carrier, which would be sailed into international waters where it could serve as a nightclub for outlaw weekenders, under no national jurisdiction. This was deemed too ambitious. However, it wasn't long before similar ideas began to cross the divide into reality.

# CHAPTER 7

**TOUR OF CORNWALL /
THE NUMBER 23 / FUZZY BIRDS /
OUTLAW HUNTING /
SOMETHING OUT OF KILLING JOKE**

The first thing Creation did after signing SFA was to send them on a short tour of Cornwall. Not the most glamorous of jaunts, but the label were thinking strategically: if the band needed to get match fit before entering the studio, they'd do their credibility the least amount of damage playing to a bunch of West Country hippies.

Despite having left the Furries some months back, Rhys Ifans enlisted himself onto the tour of Cornwall under the pseudonym of 'Tour Man Al', to see what hijinks he could get up to. As it turned out, Creation's pocket money of ten pounds a night per person was enough to buy quite a few drinks in towns like St Ives, and a week of decadent madness ensued.

On the first night, Cian and Bunf discovered a passion for tequila, chased down with the nineties alcopop Hooch. After several rounds, Bunf reached breaking point and puked through his nose, prompting the band to discreetly flee the scene. Once back at the hotel, Rhys picked up Bunf by the legs and began using him as a human lawnmower. Unfortunately this horticultural innovation backfired and Bunf cracked one of his ribs, acquiring himself the nickname Ribsy. 'If Rhys had stayed in the band, I wouldn't be here today. I'd be dead,' notes Bunf.

The next day's drinking spree started even earlier, and by late afternoon they were staggering around the harbour. 'Speedboats!' cried Rhys, pointing ahead to a rental bay and immediately heading in its direction. Guitar tech Owen Powell did not like the sound of this.

'Please! Don't do it! Don't go! You're all going to die!' he pleaded as the band got in the boat with a demented Rhys at the wheel.

'Don't worry about us, Owen, we're professional seamen now!' cackled Rhys as the boat rocked sideways like a mad buffalo, before jetting out into the ocean, leaving in its wake the distant screech of a lunatic.

Once back in Cardiff, the band got on with demo'ing their debut album, mapping out the record largely from Gruff's batch of incredible new songs.

The decision to record at Rockfield Studios in Gwent was based on several factors. Oasis had recorded *What's the Story (Morning Glory)* there – so it had good recent history – but furthermore Rockfield, although local, had been perceived by the Furries as being financially out of bounds. 'It was like an occupied castle that was rightfully ours,' says Gruff. 'It was in Wales, but all these rock dinosaurs were using it, while we had no access. We wanted to take back Rockfield!'

Until this moment, the band had been used to recording at Gorwel's house and sleeping in the van, eating pot noodles and surviving off the previous week's amphetamine binge. By contrast, at Rockfield they woke up every morning to the sound of jacuzzis being switched on, and jumped out of luxury beds like kids on Christmas Day.

The level of extravagance was both funny and bizarre: convinced they would be dropped as soon as the label came to their senses, the band started eating four hot meals a day, taking jacuzzis, bingeing on cake and blitzing whatever freebies came their way.

But they soon realised that being bloated with food made the recording process sleepy and lethargic, and songs such as 'Long Gone' started to be imbued with a sense of weary melancholy.

Meanwhile, Creation had a plan. In order to help Gorwel along, they flew their own engineer up to the studio to assist: Andy Wilkins had worked on the My Bloody Valentine album *Loveless* and was considered a safe pair of hands by the label, to whom Gorwel was a trusted but unknown quantity.

Despite all this professional help, however, the crew soon discovered that the 'big studio experience' wasn't quite what they were expecting. They'd been used to fast and spontaneous methods: back at Gorwel's home studio, if they wanted to record a drum in the garden they'd just go and do it and then come back. At Rockfield, things were done correctly, by the book – and slowly. Gorwel himself, meanwhile, sat in tears over the forty-foot mixing desk: the rawness that he so easily captured at home was proving tough to find.

'I did find some things more difficult,' he says today, 'though not all the changes were negative; working with an engineer was a great experience in many ways, as was having access to more microphones and the opportunity to record live with the degree of separation that you can't get in a small room.'

The debut album sessions were not without curious bouts of amusement. On the third day, Gruff sat down next to Gorwel in the control room. The producer was having difficulties with the twenty-third channel of his mixing desk.

'First it stops working, then it starts making these weird noises!' he grumbled.

Gruff leaned back and stared at the ceiling, preparing to doze. Then he counted twenty-three wooden beams.

'What a strange coincidence,' he murmured, shutting his eyes while Gorwel nervously stroked his chin.

Later that night Daf arrived carrying an answering machine, which appeared to contain a strange, undecipherable rant from Rhys.

'This appeared on my machine late last night,' explained Daf, shaking his head as the voice gabbled away in the background. 'He's clearly in the midst of an extreme acid frenzy.'

The band solemnly nodded their heads, then – appreciating the tape's unique nature – sampled it onto the album and moved on.

When they weren't recording, the Furries used their time to discover new sounds. During the second week, Cian came across a Fender Rhodes keyboard lying around the studio. Switching it on, he found that it made an ambient, fluid tone. Later that evening the instrument made its debut as the band worked on a new melody called 'Ice Hockey Hair' – and it would soon become a distinctive part of their sound.

Another new instrument, the balalaika, would not. It had been decided that the Russian folk instrument would match the desolate atmosphere of 'Gathering Moss', so the band dialled up a session player from their Musician's Union book. A Russian arrived the next day wearing a t-shirt that read 'I LOVE AIRPLANE RUNWAYS'. Naturally enough, Guto enquired as to what this meant.

'Well, you know those guys who protest airport expansion?' said the man. Guto nodded.

'I'm not one of them. I'm pro-airports.'

Suddenly there was a shout from upstairs that the lights had gone out. Then the ground-floor lights went out. Then the whole studio was plunged into darkness, leaving the Russian airport supporter in a confused panic. Guto ran upstairs to find Gruff looking out the window. There, out in the darkness of night, was a strange shower of sparks.

'What the fuck is it?' whispered Gruff.

'It's the twenty-third day of the month!' howled Gorwel from behind a sofa. 'We're doomed!'

The next day it all became clear: a swan had flown into a nearby power line, exploding in the process and shutting down Rockfield's electricity. Naturally the beast had croaked – but it was commemorated for posterity the next day in a song called 'Fuzzy Birds'.

It was the strange duality of the songs they were recording – that were both simple and twisted – that led to the band naming the record *Fuzzy Logic*. The phrase is traditionally a computing term, used to cover degrees of truth which can register anywhere between completely true and completely false – shades of grey, in other words.

In the studio, fuzzy logic of a different kind was manifesting itself as the band began referencing a scrapbook of heroes and pop icons, including everyone from Bunf's hamster Stavros and Ron Mael of Sparks, to the Welsh weathergirl Sian Lloyd and American stand-up comic Bill Hicks, whose leftist libertarianism appealed to SFA's taste for outlaw culture.

Another interesting tip of the hat went to the French UFO abductee Franck Fontaine. Fontaine had gone missing for several weeks in 1979, before being found one night lying in a cabbage field. A month later, while he was pouring ketchup onto his chips in a café, memories of aliens came suddenly flooding back to him. For the Furries it was a beautiful story, made even better by the fact that Fontaine had a rock-star name and shaggy, rebellious looks.

Gruff's own interest in flying saucers dated back to his childhood in Pembrokeshire, which is sometimes dubbed the 'UFO capital of Europe'. The huge number of sightings in the county was, in some small part, the singer's own fault: as a child he would hang foil discs off a clothes line and distribute photos around his classmates, causing pandemonium. Gruff was not the only source of extraterrestrial activity in Pembrokeshire, however: the Dyfed Triangle was a well-documented region of sightings in the 1970s, and Gruff's own father – a respected figure in local government, lest we forget – saw a UFO from the top of a mountain in 1971.

Alien abductees, weathergirls and rock-star comedians were all entering the vocabulary of *Fuzzy Logic*, but there was soon to be another cultural icon: a man whose infamy and subversive philosophy would appeal to the band greatly.

*Terre Haute Penitentiary, Indiana, USA.* The bearded convict sat in his cell, bathed in a ray of white sunlight that illuminated the smoke emanating from both himself and his guest. After pausing to gently consider a sheet of paper, he spoke to his visitor, a fellow convict of at least twice his weight.

'Now, Biggie, you know that they don't spell Mississippi like that.' He took the pencil and leaned towards the desk. 'Look, MI-SS-ISS-IPPI. Four Ss and two Ps. Here, have another go.'

There was a clang on the bars from behind them.

'Marks!'

'Yes, Staff Sergeant Peterson, what can we do for you?'

'You've got a CD from England. From a company called Creation Records.'

The man took a puff of smoke and raised an eyebrow. 'Creation Records?'

'Yes. It seems someone has written a song about you.'

'Well,' smiled the convict. 'I'm sorry, Mr Smalls, but it looks like we'll have to continue your writing lessons another day.'

At the time, Howard Marks was not the well-known author and speaker he is today; he was a mysterious figure whose anti-establishment antics had turned into a kind of contemporary folklore. Gruff had originally been made aware of the cannabis smuggler by a songwriter called Gareth Sion, who had written a folk track about Marks some years previously. The song was cryptic, it didn't mention Marks by name, which only added to the mystique of a man who was said to have assumed over forty different aliases during his time at large.

By 1995, the Furries were captivated by Marks' legend. His evasion of the authorities gave him the tint of a revolutionary icon; yet the Furries were also seeking a progressive Welsh archetype with an internationalist vision.

At the time, they were consciously trying to create what they termed outlaw culture, a reaction against certain notions of Welsh nationalism. This had been cemented in their minds one night when they'd visited Cardiff's music venue Club Ifor Bach, which that evening was operating a Welsh-speakers-only door policy. When the gig came to a close and Heather Jones came on to sing 'Land of My Fathers', they were disheartened to see everyone standing up to sing the national anthem. Says Gruff today, 'We made a point to sit down – we're not interested in any anthem, it's such an antiquated notion and so exclusive. We're all about inclusion.'

Certainly the band loved Wales, but precisely because they wanted to see it on the world stage they rejected the inward-looking, nationalist school of thought. Amid these cultural complications, it was time to seek guidance from somebody who'd created their own politics rather than getting sucked into somebody else's.

Over at Creation, the label's marketing guru John Andrews was listening to the latest tapes from Rockfield. He spotted 'Hanging with Howard Marks' on the tracklisting and remembered the band's vocal admiration for the convict.

Andrews stroked his chin and picked up the phone. 'Anderson. Find out which prison Howard Marks is in. What? It's an American federal *penitentiary*? Shit. OK, listen up. I'm going to get you a demo and I want it posted out to Marks asap. And find out when he's getting released!'

That June, the Furries received a strange fax. It was a guestlist request for their next gig, at Pontypridd Town Hall, which simply read 'Howard Marks +10.'

The legendary dope smuggler had only been out of prison for two months when he showed up at the gig, apparently wearing the same clothes he'd been busted in back in 1988: a Michael Jackson-style red jacket, leather trousers and a black cape. As Gruff later noted, 'He looked like something out of Killing Joke.'

Marks was on fine form, however, cheerfully telling stories about taking on the FBI and recommending the health benefits of yoga. At the aftershow party, he sat down with Rhys Ifans to share a drink and reminisce. 'I wanna play you in a film one day!' said Rhys, in awe of the charismatic ex-fugitive.

# CHAPTER 8
## FIRED FROM A CANNON /
## HANGING WITH HOWARD MARKS /
## MEET THE PRESS / BAZ

By the mid nineties, graphic designer Brian Cannon had created some of the most recognisable record sleeves of the Britpop boom, including Oasis's *Definitely Maybe*, Suede's *Dog Man Star* and The Verve's *A Northern Soul*. There was, however, one job he wasn't quite expecting.

'Right, Brian, listen up. I've signed a new band called the Super Furry Animals. How would you like to make their first pop video?'

On the other end of the phone, Cannon was overwhelmed. 'Alan? I take my hat off to you, mate. I'm bang up for it!' McGee had clearly decided that if Brian could design classic record sleeves, he could damn well shoot a video too.

With characteristic enthusiasm Cannon signed up for the role. Says Gruff: 'He came to Wales and learned Welsh overnight, copped off with a Welsh woman, threw himself into the language – this was all over the period of a week. He launched himself into our lives.'

Motivational and energetic, Brian immediately clicked with the band during the shoot for 'Hometown Unicorn'. Says Cannon today: 'If I'm into something I'm bang into it – it becomes infectious, like "Fucking come on – get on this!" And after a while they realised that I wouldn't necessarily be excited about something that's a bad idea, so they went with me.'

By the time the shoot had wrapped, Cannon was at the centre of his own creative tornado. Drinking in Cardiff on the final night, he announced: 'If I'm not doing your album cover I'll take it as a personal insult!'

As it happened, the idea was already taking shape: Gruff had sourced a collection of Howard Marks passport photos from the *Guardian* photo library, each one depicting the criminal mastermind in different disguises. The original plan had been to use them for the inner sleeve of the record. It was Cannon who placed the photos on a table and arranged them into a collage with his fingers, before declaring, 'Fucking hell, I can see a record sleeve there!'

At around the same time, Creation's marketing guru John Andrews had learned that Marks was gearing up to release his autobiography, *Mr Nice*. In an inspired publicity move, Andrews started to make the necessary phone calls to ensure that *Fuzzy Logic* would hit the shops simultaneously with the book. The plan was simple: to invade the zeitgeist with a double whammy.

Warming to the idea, Creation's press officer Andy Saunders decided that the band should visit Howard at his Spanish home in Majorca, with a music journalist from the *NME* in tow. This wasn't just a publicity stunt: Howard had closely bonded with the band back in Wales, sharing both a common first language and an appreciation of mischief. The invitation to visit him at home had been open ever since the night at Pontypridd Town Hall.

As soon as the doors of the plane opened and the heat of Majorca wafted in, the Furries and their crew immediately began microwaving in their jeans. 'Welcome to the Mediterranean!' shouted Andy Saunders at the panicked Celts. 'We'll buy some shorts on the way!'

Once freshened up, the band were greeted by Howard at his

villa – and the famous smuggler immediately put his foot on the gas to show them the beauty of the town. From the clubs of Magaluf to the mountaintop parties of Deià, it was a luxurious wonderland.

During a trip to the latter mountains, the band discovered a community of ex-pat stoners. Some were ageing hippies who'd lived in the mountains since the sixties, others were posh, wannabe criminals who used their family yachts to smuggle things about. On Cian's twenty-first birthday, the band were at a flamenco dance party when a moustached man on their table began whispering about a massive counterfeiting operation he'd just gotten away with. He had, he said, forged millions of dollars.

'And guess how I got away with it?' grinned the man. 'I stamped all the bills *"In dog we trust"*! You get it? In *dog* we trust? The FBI couldn't believe it! They couldn't bust me! Ha ha ha!'

During these four days, the Furries discovered that Howard Marks was incredibly energetic. They'd stay up all night and go to bed at 5am, only to find Howard in their bedrooms two hours later, announcing a trip to the coast.

They also found pause for reflection. Gruff in particular had been relatively settled before the band had been signed, and although he was excited about the imminent Furrymania, he was finding it difficult to adjust to their unpredictable lifestyle. On the final night, he sat up with Howard overlooking the twinkling lights of Majorca from a poolside bar.

'Listen, Gruff,' said the older man, putting a hand on the singer's shoulder. 'The greatest human asset is enthusiasm – you've got to approach this thing with enthusiasm. It's the greatest thing you could possibly have! Let that be the governing force of any decision you make.'

Four months later, the Brit Awards were underway in London: paparazzi, celebrities, red carpets and rock stars, Michael Jackson and Jarvis Cocker, David Bowie and the Pet Shop Boys. The big winners of the night were Oasis, whose record *What's the Story (Morning Glory)* was set to win Best Album and Best Artwork. When the artwork award was announced, however, Liam Gallagher looked around their table. Their designer was missing.

'Where the fuck is Brian?'

Meanwhile, in the countryside just outside Derby, a van sped over the hills carrying the Super Furry Animals, their tour manager, and Brian Cannon – who was screaming battle cries out of the window. The band were on a national tour with the power-pop trio Bis, and Cannon had run away to join the circus.

It was a heady time: one night Thom Yorke would turn up at a show, the next the band would be flown to an obscure European city just to do an interview. The Furries soon realised how much they still had to learn about handling the media when, during their first trip to a regional radio station, they watched Craig David in action through the studio glass.

'I'm Craig David, and you're listening to GWR FM,' the singer purred in one smooth take. If his savvy delivery had raised nervous eyebrows, however, it wasn't long before the band grew confident enough to begin pranking the media. During an interview, a French journalist commented on the ridiculously long title of their debut EP.

'That's why it was recognised,' said Daf with a straight face, 'by *Guinness World Records* as being the longest EP name of all time.'

The following week the band were back in the UK, sat before a young music hack from the *Independent*. 'So how did it feel to be recognised by the *Guinness Book of Records*?' he asked. 'You guys must feel pretty proud, right?'

Once they had a taste for it, media manipulation became a regular source of amusement. Yet it also became a way of puncturing the lazy clichés of the British music press – that Welsh-speaking people came from misty valleys, hung out with flute-playing goats and ate magic mushrooms for breakfast. Rather than be patronised by these misconceptions, the band opted for a policy of KLF-style myth-making and subversion. Nonetheless, they remained on guard: they were meeting the press at a time when it was still deemed acceptable to crack sheep-shagging jokes, and their contemporaries in the Manic Street Preachers had attracted xenophobic, sometimes politically motivated abuse. The Furries went in feet first, with Daf taking their first *NME* interviewer to one side and delivering a blunt, don't-fuck-with-us warning.

That May, *Fuzzy Logic* hit number twenty-three in the charts, much to Gorwel's horror. The record had given the Super Furries their first experience of what they came to describe as 'demo-itis': a suspicion that the original demos had captured the spirit of the songs better than their final studio counterparts. The band vowed to retain that spark of instantaneous creation on all future recordings.

Despite being viewed by the band as something of a missed opportunity, *Fuzzy Logic* sold well, and came to be acclaimed by *Q* magazine as one of the best British albums of all time. It stands today as an upbeat collection of great singles tied together with moments of puppyish optimism ('For Now and Ever'), subversive punk rock ('Bad Behaviour'), existential pathos ('Gathering Moss') and casually futuristic Nintendo-pop ('Mario Man') – the last of which would provide a clue as to where the band would go next. Perhaps the best indicator that *Fuzzy Logic* had succeeded, meanwhile, came from the other side of the world, when a tribute band, the Australian Super Furry Animals, formed in Perth.

Once Creation's co-founder Dick Green had chosen 'If You Don't Want Me to Destroy You' as the next single, the band's marketing guru John Andrews called one of his infamous pub meetings.

'OK, lads, the new single's on the way and we've got a few grand in the bank. What shall we go with? Full page in the *NME*? Billboards?'

Daf went into a state of deep thought. The drummer had harboured an obsession with tanks since he was nine, and even attempted to build one in his dad's shed. So when someone offered him a couple of grand to spend on whatever he liked, there was only one realistic answer. John Andrews took notes and nodded as Daf explained why buying a tank was a really good idea. Then he looked up and smiled. 'Leave it with me.'

The next week, John was back on the phone. 'OK, I've made contact with an arms dealer in Nottingham. He's selling a tank for ten grand, which is frankly more than our budget . . . But, if we sell it back at the end of the festival season, we can sell it for *eight* grand, so overall it'll only cost two grand. In other words, I think we can get one.'

'Great! This arms dealer . . . is he reliable?'

'Who, Baz?'

'His name's Baz?'

'Er, yes, but . . . listen, everything will be fine. I'll see you on Saturday morning. Don't be late.'

They pulled up outside the iron gates of the Nottingham industrial estate, and pressed the intercom button. It was cold. It was quiet. They considered running away – but then came the voice.

'Who's there?'

'Hello, Baz?' said John, suddenly aware of how damned polite he sounded. 'This is John Andrews from Creation Records. May we come in, please?'

There was no answer, but then the metal gates slowly creaked open. Their car cruised nervously forwards for another thirty feet, then Daf looked up and pointed.

'There!'

A middle-aged man in an eye patch was hobbling towards them from the direction of a metal cabin. This was the guy.

'We've got a wide range of amphibious vehicles, as you can see,' explained Baz, walking the band through a huge courtyard containing amphibian submarines and deep-sea body suits. 'We've also got a special offer on MiG fighter jets, if you're interested.'

'Fighter jets?' said Guto.

John swiftly formed a human barrier between them.

'We're just here for the tanks, thank you.'

Thirty minutes later, John waved out of his car window as they pulled through the gates once again. They hadn't bonded with Baz, and wouldn't be keeping in touch, but they had just bought a refurbished Second World War army tank off of him: not bad for a group of committed pacifists.

Cian, meanwhile, was still thinking about those amphibian submarines. 'Next year,' he muttered.

The tank was immediately customised to the band's specifications. Its primary function would be as a mobile soundsystem that could challenge the Criminal Justice Act: on the outside, speakers were welded to the steel so they couldn't be removed. On the inside, the decks, amplifiers and controls were installed, effectively sealing them off from legal seizure and protecting the DJ from arrest. Meanwhile if the authorities tried to remove the tank . . . well, it was a tank. There was only one final specification to be made: Cian recommended that the soundsystem should be as loud as Creation's budget could afford.

Following a chaotic test-drive at Eisteddfod Llandeilo, the Super Furry tank made its next scheduled appearance at a VW Beetle weekender, where it began to dawn on Cian that his new DJ booth was not without its challenges. Halfway through his set, a drop of oil suddenly landed on the vinyl and began spinning round. The DJ stroked his jaw and muttered to himself, then set about mixing the tune out before the needle reached the blob. Then a second drop hit the record at an entirely different point.

'Ah, shit!' he cursed.

Oil blobs successfully navigated, the techno set kicked in and Cian began to sit back and enjoy himself. But then something even weirder happened: the entire vehicle started gently bobbing from side to side. As soon as he'd dropped the next record, Cian picked up the walkie-talkie and radioed over to Daf.

'What the fuck is going on?'

'There are about fifty people dancing on top of you!' laughed his brother from the other side of the field. 'That thing must weigh over seventeen tons and they're rocking it all over the place!'

The tank turned out to be the best £2,000 the band ever spent. Beyond the media coverage that it generated, it also spawned a thousand myths and stories, as people talked of the time they clambered aboard the 'techno tank' for a dance. Perhaps above all, it sent out a message of attitude that resounded somewhere between the freewheeling subversion of the Merry Pranksters and the dream-out-loud publicity stunts of the KLF.

'Everybody thought I'd say no to the tank,' says Alan McGee today, 'but I like the idea of being bizarre, ridiculous – so me being me, I said yes. They terrorised the festivals, got away with murder. Nobody could repatriate the tank.'

As festival season came to a close, John Andrews reluctantly met his half of the bargain and had the vehicle returned to Baz's compound. Before leaving, he casually enquired as to who its next owner was to be.

'Don Henley,' croaked the arms dealer, closing his books.

'Don Henley from The Eagles?' spluttered John.

'That's the one.'

It seemed that Daf wasn't the only rock star with a thing for tanks.

If their Criminal Justice Act-busting soundsystem had indicated that SFA had a taste for anti-establishment activities, their next single would confirm it. Alan McGee had spent the weekend in his London flat listening to the Furries' next single and its B-side. The only thing was he couldn't stop playing the B-side. In fact, that weekend he played 'The Man Don't Give a Fuck' over thirty times, becoming increasingly addicted. On Monday morning he got on the phone to Dick Green.

'Why aren't we releasing "The Man Don't Give a Fuck" as the next single?'

'It's the Steely Dan sample,' said Dick. 'We haven't got clearance on it.'

'Fuck Steely Dan, let's give them the money!'

An hour later, McGee was writing a cheque for £2,500 and the band were being phoned about Creation's decision. As McGee put it to them: 'You're on the label that doesn't give a fuck, too. We're putting it out.' At first the band were in disagreement with McGee's idea: they figured there was no way the radio would touch this single. And they didn't. Yet the release proved to be a thrilling, anarchistic statement that sealed the deal for countless Furry fans, while entering the record books as the pop song that used the word 'fuck' more times than any other.

The title of the single, as well as the sentiment behind it, would come to be commonly misinterpreted: it was the establishment that didn't give a fuck – not the band. As *NME* journalist Alan Woodhouse recalls: 'Guto once told me that a t-shirt company wanted to print shirts with the slogan "SFA – We Don't Give a Fuck", which, as he rightly pointed out, was missing the point of the song entirely. It still sounds amazing – trust them to make such a perceptive comment on the world in such a wonderfully warped manner.'

The Furries weren't averse to meddling with the perception of the statement themselves, however: they saw out Christmas 1996 by dedicating 'The Man Don't Give a Fuck' to the memory of Cardiff City's legendary footballer Robin Friday, placing an image of the troubled player flicking the Vs on the cover and commending his 'stand against "The Man"'. Who exactly was not giving a fuck in this context was admirably ambiguous – fuzzy logic indeed.

1996 had flashed before their eyes in a blizzard of touring, hedonism, strange wisdoms and stranger noise. Yet just as quickly the noise fell silent, and the Furries found themselves under the still skies of South Wales, demo'ing new songs. As dazed and confused as returned alien abductees, they began preparing their second album: it was January 1997, and time to show the world what they could do.

# CHAPTER 9

**TURNING JAPANESE /
F-16 JETSTREAMS / CIAN-DO-ATTITUDE /
OFF THE MAP**

The Furries were in Spillers Records in Cardiff when they noticed the fanzine. 'Now *that's* what an album cover should look like!' said Bunf, pointing to its cover art – a painting of a Japanese girl walking out of a sex shop.

The image struck a perfect chord with the ideas the band had accumulated in Japan while on tour in '96, ideas that were further impressed upon them by tour partners Bis, an indie trio with a distinct *kawaii* image. By a strange twist of fate, the artist behind this painting had been tuning into the exact same frequencies.

'I was starting to spend more time in Japan, being influenced by everything from their toys to just the whole Japanese popular culture,' says Pete Fowler. 'I was touching on ancient myths that are still alive in the country, despite the fact they're very technologically advanced and forward-looking.'

Pete had been contributing artwork to *GQ* and putting his work out through flyers and psychedelic all-nighters when he was asked for an interview with a young, Cardiff-based writer called Bethan Elfyn. He immediately agreed to the feature and cover design of her underground paper, having no idea of what it would lead to. 'I was quite lucky,' he says. 'You put yourself out there and you don't realise how far it's gone, or who it's been seen by.'

At first, the band assumed that the painter was probably Japanese, but when they found out he was actually from Cardiff their curiosity doubled, and Creation were alerted. A week later, John Andrews was on the phone to Pete.

'The band has seen your work in Wales, in this Welsh magazine . . .'

'Oh yeah, I know what that is.'

'We'd like to see if you could bike your book over?'

'Great!'

Pete was already a fan of the band's music, so when his folio was given the thumbs up, he was excited. However, when he met the Furries the following week and realised that he was to be given full creative freedom, he couldn't believe his luck. At one of John Andrews' pub meetings, Gruff handed him a handwritten sheet of paper.

'They're the names of demos for the next album,' explained the singer, 'although these might not end up actually being the titles, so if you get inspiration from them then great, but otherwise . . . do what you want!'

Pete was immediately impressed by the band's friendliness and relative lack of ego. 'As soon as I met up with them we got on really well; shared music tastes, similar outlooks: that made it a lot easier,' he says. 'I walked away from the meeting thinking, well this is a bit weird – I thought they'd have had a really strong idea about what they wanted! It was very popular at the time for bands to have photo covers, and I don't think the guys were really into that. They wanted something to visually represent their music rather than a photograph of them.'

As Pete returned to his studio and began to think more about Japanese mythology, the band started a journey of their own into the cool mists of North Wales. It was time to record an album.

\*

The Furries arrived at Gorwel's coastal studio in Anglesey on the same night that the Hale-Bopp comet passed over, its blue tail glittering magically in the cosmos. It was a breathless start to a project that had been conceptualised as a return to hands-on record making: the band knew Gorwel's place inside out and could work quickly there, maintaining complete control.

The studio is situated at the bottom of an RAF runway, and the band would freshen themselves up every morning by standing below the flight path of fighter jets as they roared overhead. It became a popular sport to flick the Vs at the pilots as they flew over, and laugh as the pilots flicked the Vs right back.

Down the road, a local neighbour had overheard something about famous rock stars visiting the area, so he made the entrepreneurial decision to lease out his converted barn as 'celebrity accommodation'. With three bedrooms, there was at least the option to keep Daf's snoring confined while the others split the remaining rooms between them. It was nonetheless an intimate experience.

With three months booked up for recording and Cardiff five hours away by road, *Radiator* went into production within its own, isolated microclimate. On the one hand this generated sharp focus: Gruff began to plaster the wall of his bedroom with notes, news clippings and ideas. 'It was one of the most intense times for lyrics I've ever been through,' he says today. 'I was re-writing songs ten times before getting the lyrics right.'

Although Gorwel was happy to be back in his home studio, he'd learned a lot recording *Fuzzy Logic* and already had an inkling of which direction the band's second record would take.

'I think I saw *Radiator* as part of a long progression rather than a fundamental shift,' he says. 'Some of the B-sides that we recorded for the first album formed a kind of bridge into it, especially "Arnofio/Glô in the Dark".'

Despite the sharp focus on the work, some band members began to worry that every passing day brought the prospect of being dumped by their girlfriends in Cardiff that little bit closer. After several weeks of recording, Gruff suggested they take some time out to go and watch Beck play in the capital city.

'Aren't we supposed to be making a record here?' questioned Gorwel, insisting that they stick to the road map.

'OK,' conceded Gruff, 'but I really should see my girlfriend soon or it's going to be over!'

The producer was understanding but kept his eye firmly on the bigger picture. 'Maintaining focus is difficult when working away from a partner for a long period of time,' he concedes today. 'I guess that, looking back, there probably was a lot to do in terms of keeping things moving and keeping track of what needed doing, though I can't say it felt like that at the time and working with SFA was always very much a collaborative effort.'

Gruff's emotional insecurities manifested themselves in a few of the songs: 'Download' speaks of *losing our friends, who will number but few* in the *corporate rush to devour the new*, while 'Carry the Can' is a weary expression of self-doubt that verges on the hopeless: *'Evolution stops right here with me . . . my descendants will be fish.'*

Because it was so dreary, 'Carry the Can' was cut. The Furries had noticed a recent trend for bleak-sounding indie bands complaining about their rock-star existences, and they wanted no part of it. Here were five close friends, signed to a great label, recording an album at a time of unprecedented popularity for independent bands; to moan about it would have seemed outrageous.

Instead, *Radiator* was conceived as a euphoric, multicolour pop record that would react not just against miserable music, but also against the band's own feeling that their debut album had played it too safe. Immediately they set about compressing complex ideas into pop timeframes, allowing the SFA Soundsystem techniques to infiltrate some of their strongest songs to date. As Gorwel now says, 'I think it would have been quite difficult not to make *Radiator* an exceptional record, bearing in mind the strength of the material.'

The band's evolution towards a more radical sound owed a huge amount to Cian. Back when Creation had given the band a £20,000 advance, he'd bought an MPC sampler which, although it had lain dormant in its box for a while, he had mastered by the time the Furries returned to Gorwel's. He could now write complex digital sequences alongside the primary colours of rock and roll – drums, bass, guitar – and then refine his ideas with the band's input between sessions, as he explains: 'I would say "Listen to this, what do you think? Does this work?" and they might say "Yes, but not throughout the entire song, let's change it at the end."'

Cian's new-found skills would come to bookend *Radiator*. On its first track, 'Placid Casual', he surprised everyone by revealing himself as a pianist, using the Rhodes piano to create a gorgeous dawn-like feeling. Later, the LP climaxes to the sound of his techno fireworks exploding in their box, during 'Mountain People'.

'There was an opportunity to develop "Mountain People" at the end because it was so monotonous, in a good way,' Cian explains. 'Most techno or house tracks are repetitive. Some people find it annoying, but the point is it takes you into a trance.'

Throughout the recording process, Cian's programming started to take on the voice of a malfunctioning R2-D2, slotting between the electric guitars with mischievous futurism on tracks like 'The International Language of Screaming'.

With a programmer and pianist now in their ranks, the Furries found themselves shifted back in their element as a radical band, experimenting with minute details of the record. At one point,

Gorwel persuaded Bunf to record twenty-four samples of E-bow manipulated guitar, so that, with a different sample assigned to each channel, the mixing desk could be played like a giant keyboard to create chords. Meanwhile, Cian installed his decks in the studio and began to blast out drum 'n' bass sets, transforming Gorwel's studio into a high-octane, creative factory.

At the same time, the band's energies were being fuelled by an unlikely source. 'Gorwel's friend would provide a huge bowl of carrots for us every day,' says Bunf. 'She was being paid to feed us more and more carrots.'

Whether the carrots had anything to do with it or not, the band started to produce some strange, otherworldly music. 'Hermann Loves Pauline' is primarily a song about Albert Einstein's parents, Marie Curie and the heyday of physics, while 'Torra Fy Ngwallt Yn Hir' is a song in which the narrator repeatedly begs for a haircut.

For all the surrealism of Gruff's themes, however, there are also plenty of clear insights to be found: *'Every time I look around me everything seems so stationary / It just sends me the impulse to become reactionary,'* the singer declares during 'The International Language of Screaming' – a sentiment that goes some way to explaining his ceaseless creativity. The phrase 'international language of screaming' itself, meanwhile, was a response to critics of the band in Wales who had portrayed them as unpatriotic for singing in English.

'People were asking us a lot about language at the time,' Gruff recalls, 'and ultimately rock and roll is a primal medium, where it's all about emotion. So it doesn't matter what you're saying, or what language you're saying it in; what people connect to is a deep human emotion. Like a scream!'

Speaking later to the music newspaper *Melody Maker*, Daf explained that the group wasn't biased towards one language or another – they were simply pro-communication. 'We wanna see English as just another language in pop. Not *the* language. Hopefully, in a few years' time there'll be African number ones and Japanese number ones,' he said, before adding prophetically: 'You've got computers and email and mobiles and satellites on the way. Geography is coming apart at the seams. You'll get bands coming from Tunisia soon!'

Despite the Furries' determination to keep the LP as positive as possible, the long wintery nights of Anglesey eventually influenced them in subtle, reflective ways. 'We were going through an emotional time,' says Gruff now. '"Demons" is about a relationship falling apart, and trying to keep a lid on demonic forces that are going to destroy you and trying to cope with them! It's also about living outside structures, like the idea of fuzzy logic – there's no black and white, it's just fuzz. It's about the grey area.'

Demons of a different kind, meanwhile, stalked 'Down a Different River'. In the song, Gruff addresses a cokehead whose endless stream of gibberish is fast becoming a bum trip. *'Oh won't you tell it to someone else?'* he asks, craving hibernation from a relentless conveyor belt of excess. SFA had never been shy of referencing drugs in their songs, yet they had also realised that becoming stereotyped as acid-munching hedonists would do their music no favours – and, as 'Down a Different River' shows, they were all too aware that cocaine could inspire crazed egotism. In keeping with their refusal to cave in to miserablism, however, 'Down a Different River' evolves into one of the album's standout tracks, breaking out of its dusky acoustics into an insistently forward-looking chorus.

After three months of isolation, the Super Furries finally decided to haul the tapes from Anglesey to Parr Street in Liverpool, where they could be sculpted into an album. In selecting the tracklisting, they stayed true to their vision of emphasising the upbeat tracks, and in doing so ensured that the first two-thirds of *Radiator* would whoosh forwards with the momentum of the F-16s they'd been waking up to. The result is that, by the time the record hits its ninth track, 'Chupacabras' – a speed punk number about a notorious Mexican vampire goat – it feels as unstoppably euphoric as a World Cup match.

There was, however, one other reason why *Radiator* was about to light the fuse of Furrymania: by recording it, the band had invented a sound far more radical than anything coming from the sixties-obsessed Britpop guitar bands. If the aim had been to rebel against the traditional nature of their debut, they'd not only succeeded, but also zoomed straight past the target, landing somewhere completely off the map.

# CHAPTER 10
## PAINTING DEMONS /
## BOUNCY CASTLE LICENCE /
## S4C ON THE ATTACK/OVERTAKEN BY A WHEEL

For every day that the Furries had spent sculpting their demos into the best fuzz-pop record they could muster, Pete Fowler had been brainstorming to them, sketching to them, and finally painting to them. The canvases that he eventually delivered depicted a parallel universe of shaggy-haired subversives, where techno-savvy agents and cute-but-evil monsters populated the city; where vampires smoked coolly outside nightclubs; and where demonic doppelgängers were only a shop window reflection away.

As expected, Japanese pop culture had infiltrated the mix. Ideas of myth and duality in particular proved compelling for Fowler, who took particular enjoyment in exploring the notion that a character could be at once cuddly and sinister. Technology proved to be an additional Japanese influence, and one that would have long-standing ramifications for both Pete and the band. One of the artist's souvenirs from the country had been an early digital camera; but it wasn't the functional side of the contraption that appealed to him as much as the sheer shape of the thing.

'I'd grown up on *2000AD* and was really into sci-fi, so it was like "This is the future!"' he says.

On returning from Japan, Pete noticed that all his friends were starting to buy mobile phones. And, as with the digital camera, it was their futuristic shapes that caught the designer's attention. 'It was almost like a fetishistic object,' he says. 'There were these Motorola M3s, these Eriksons with big rubber aerials – I really loved the objects.'

Consequently, the characters in Pete's paintings appeared armed with handsets: sometimes literally, with the phones strapped to their chests as if they were rubbery grenades. The mobile phone revolution wouldn't become a mass-market phenomenon for another couple of years but, like Pete, the band were fascinated; mobile handsets seemed to them an extension of the idea they'd enthused about on 'The International Language of Screaming', that communication was the key to empowerment, the great blitzer of boundaries.

The more Pete worked on his paintings, the more they all started to merge into one surreal, comic book-style collection, to the extent that any one of them would make a fantastic record cover. His lack of preconceptions meant that, when he arrived at Creation Records carrying five canvases, he could sit back and enjoy the process as the band started pairing them with songs.

'It was cool to be able to flip these things around, almost like shuffling cards,' Pete recalls. 'Usually you're making images for a specific thing, but they were able to move them around, and I felt really comfortable with that.'

The shuffling happened quickly. A painting that depicted two laughing, hairy and plausibly stoned cavemen was assigned to 'The International Language of Screaming', despite having been inspired by a song that hadn't survived from demo to album; the portrait of a Japanese mafioso with vampire fangs was delegated to 'Demons', while the picture Pete had imagined might go well with 'Demons' became the album cover. And that was that.

A month later, Pete was driving through the car park of a Bethesda music festival where SFA were due to headline. It was a sunny afternoon, and he smiled as he drove. Then he hit the brakes. The car skidded. He blinked a few times and got out of the vehicle – walking carefully sideways with his head tilted towards the sky. Up there, from behind some tall trees, a fifty-foot monster was slowly moving into view: a huge red bear with demonic eyes strapped behind a Zorro mask, its polyester belly gently but powerfully breathing in the sun. The monster's creator took a few moments to take this in – then paused for a quiet laugh. His painting had travelled further than just the album cover; it had morphed into reality.

It had all started at one of John Andrews' notorious pub meetings.

'OK, chaps, we've two grand in the bank – those Oasis albums have been selling very nicely indeed – and it's time to whip up a marketing campaign for *Radiator*. Let's have a look at the cover then!'

Gruff handed John the artwork, which depicted a cartoon bear strolling through a city with a drink in his hand. The bear was looking at his reflection in a shop window, which depicted an evil version of himself, with pointed ears, lizard eyes and a skull logo on his cola cup.

'Nice artwork . . . *very* nice!' said John. 'So what did you want to do with the bears again?'

'Well,' said Bunf, slurping on a margarita, 'the idea is that we have life-sized versions of the good and evil bears on stage with us, during the tour. What do you think?'

'I don't see why not,' said John, stroking his chin. 'Perhaps they could even be inflatable balloons. Tell you what,' he said getting up, 'give me twenty-four hours and I'll let you know. Now I've got to get out of here. Anyone else for another margarita before I go?'

\*

The next day, John called Furry HQ in Cardiff. 'Good news, guys: we can afford the bears!'

Gruff held the phone away and relayed the news to the band, who let out a small cheer.

John continued. 'And in fact it was curious, because as I was talking to the inflatables company, they mentioned that it would cost exactly the same price for an eight-foot balloon as it would be for a *fifty*-foot balloon! Can you believe it? Naturally I told her that . . . er . . .' John noticed that the line had gone quiet.

'Gruff?'

There was mumbling in the background. Mumbling, followed by another small cheer. Gruff returned to the call.

'John?' said the singer. 'I think we'll take the large bears.'

The following week, the bears were hand delivered in their crates to Creation, from where the band and John Andrews excitedly took them down to Primrose Hill. Once there, a pair of jet-powered steel burners were hooked up to the first bear – the evil one with the Zorro mask – and Gruff grinned as he prepared to pull the chain that would inject life into the creature. But then, suddenly, a cry came from over the hill.

'Wait!' John Andrews looked up to see a junior A&R scout, apparently in some kind of panic.

'Stop!' he shouted, staggering towards them. 'We just got a call from the council. They're aware of what we're up to and phoned to see if we've got a bouncy castle licence . . .'

John Andrews raised an eyebrow. 'What the fuck is a bouncy castle licence?'

'That's beside the point – we'll almost certainly be arrested if we inflate without one.'

Daf, sensing a publicity blitz, clapped his hands together. 'Even better! Pull the chain, Gruff!'

'Wait!' shouted John, moving between Gruff and the chain.

'We have to take this seriously: if you inflate that bouncy castle it could spell the end of Creation.'

The band looked at one another, suddenly aware of the gravity of the situation. After a second's pause, Bunf quietly spoke. 'It's not a bouncy castle, John. It's a bear.'

'I know it's a fucking bear!'

A week later, the band found themselves on more inflatable-friendly ground. One of the first gigs that had been booked to celebrate the release of *Radiator* was a massive outdoor show in the epicentre of Cardiff. The gig allowed the band to invite like-minded acts such as The Fall to come along and play what was essentially a Furry festival in a giant blue circus tent.

On the morning of the show, the same jet-powered steel burners were hooked up to the good and evil bears, and the inflating commenced. 'We had to have a few mates down to watch the balloons,' says Guto today, 'because these things are dangerous: they have to be tied down. The first time we blew them up they looked amazing. And Creation loved that sort of thing, because it was good for press.'

As the blue sky faded into violet night around the fifty-foot bears, thousands of Furry fans began flocking into the big top. Inside, SFA revealed a show that was painted in brighter colours than ever before. Bunf appeared with an inflatable thinking cloud over his head, while Gruff had a light bulb hovering over his, as if he'd just thought of a great idea. Musically, almost all of *Radiator*'s experimental detail had been punched into their set, with the techno ending of 'Mountain People' in particular evolving into an extended dance music sequence, decorated with waves of space noise and a sample of Arnold Schwarzenegger declaring: 'Best mindfuck yet.'

That the Furries appeared to be having so much fun was all

the more impressive for the fact that they'd recently been the target of a televised character assassination. The Welsh-language station S4C had aired a hastily assembled documentary about the band, attacking them for singing in English and accusing them of spreading the language like some sort of zombie plague. One interviewee went as far as to accuse them of being 'the sons of Thatcher', reasoning that, because the Furries had grown up during the reign of the notoriously greed-empowering prime minister, they had no sense of social responsibility. Another scene depicted innocent teenagers driving over the Severn Bridge that separates England and Wales, only to have the music on their car radio suddenly become distorted and infected with the pernicious English language.

Though a ramshackle affair, the broadcast did manage to trigger off some debate among daytime TV commentators and local politicians, none of whom had apparently listened to the band's music. Today, Guto recalls the documentary as being 'dark and foreboding', but ultimately nothing that caused the band to sweat. 'We've only ever had shit off people in the media who wouldn't be into our band anyway – they're just looking for a hoo-ha.'

Indeed, the band had never even debated the ethics of singing in English; it simply wasn't an issue for them. 'For us, it was as easy as walking across the road,' says Bunf. 'Our Welsh-speaking bands had broken up around the same time and we just thought, let's try something in English. Imagine if Germany was the hub of rock music: maybe we'd all be writing German rock music, because that would be the norm. And it just so happens that you're brought up listening to American and English pop – it's all just a melting pot.'

Super Furry Animals were not the only people finding S4C a little hard to get on with: their former label Ankst had spelled out their disdain for the TV station by releasing a compilation titled *S4C Makes Me Want to Smoke Crack*. As Emyr Glyn Williams explains, it wasn't a cheap shot.

'The Welsh-language protest movement is probably one of the most successful protest movements in the whole of Europe, but they mightn't necessarily have felt that their sacrifice was worthwhile when they saw something like a Disney channel, pumping out a Welsh culture that seemed a bit mediocre and crap.

'If there was one channel in the whole world that could take risks and was expected to forge its own path, then S4C would have been that channel – but it didn't do it. It copied formats, chat shows and what have you – it was very tame. And Welsh culture didn't come from something tame, it came from a strong sense of independence, its own clear voice and the idea that there is a fight involved in a lot of things – to create and be heard.'

While other groups might have responded to the TV special with a defensive press conference, the Furries merely accelerated their creativity and moved on. There was, however, one piece of evidence that suggested the band were indeed allied with the forces of evil: in the final hour of their Cardiff festival, the good bear started hissing air from its knee. Within an hour the fifty-foot beast had limped over sideways, like a malfunctioning King Kong. By the time SFA's largely teenage audience began to flock out of the tent, it had collapsed entirely, prompting a mass cheering. The next day, the good bear was put into premature retirement, leaving its demonic counterpart to continue the tour alone.

As they hit the road again, the group began cultivating an addiction to football video games. It was perhaps unsurprising, then, that the makers of their favourite Playstation game – *Actua Soccer* – contacted them with a proposal. The pitch was simple: they would develop a special version of the game in which the band would appear as pixellated players. The band could then use in-game footage for their next video, 'Play It Cool'.

Galvanised by the offer, the Furries signed up immediately – although they didn't quite get what they expected.

'The five of us appeared on a team,' remembers Daf today, 'but then, without telling us, they made all the other players the biggest dictators from history.'

Suddenly the band were being depicted playing on the same football team as Attila the Hun, Genghis Khan, Stalin and Hitler. It was, to say the least, a perplexing sight. 'I was looking at this,' says Daf, 'and thinking "What the *fuck*?"'[4]

The tour continued to deliver short, sharp shocks to their heads. During one journey towards Ipswich, Bunf noticed a curious thing speeding past the window: their rear wheel. Within seconds, the van began drifting towards the hard shoulder, while the wheel continued its solo journey towards Norwich.

As winter encroached the perils of touring began to manifest themselves in strange, dangerous ways. Without the band's knowledge, Creation had assigned them a driver who was addicted to speed – and prone to taking spur-of-the-moment, unpredictable risks.

During one particularly snowy night when the band were all asleep, the driver grew frustrated with heavy traffic on the motorway to Aberdeen, and decided to take a shortcut through a wildlife sanctuary park. Shortly afterwards the band were awoken by the sound of wheels skidding in thick snow. In answer to their polite enquiries as to what was going on, the driver informed them that they were snowbound in a safari park, with large and potentially dangerous animals on the loose. Sensing that he had caused

---

[4] If you have a copy of *Actua Soccer 2*, you can play as Super Furry Animals by entering the following code: left, left, square, right, right, circle, up, down.

unnecessary fear in the band, the driver made amends by breaking into their own merchandise stall to seize some 'SFA'-emblazoned silver bomber jackets, and handing them out. Cold and afraid, the band put the jackets on – but even these were useless against the elements.

'It dawned on us that in two or three hours we'd literally be frozen,' says Bunf. 'It was the most traumatic experience of my life. We were basically fucked.'

Suddenly the dark sky was pierced by the headlights of a passing tractor, on its way to make a hay delivery.

'Get that tractor!' demanded Daf, weeping with relief.

From that day on, the Furries resolved to take no more risks: they demanded a silver-bullet bus, a bar, bunk beds and a driver who was not addicted to speed.

# CHAPTER II

**RISE OF THE SHINTO GODS /
AIR PANIC / GRINGOS IN THE MIST /
UNBRIDLED FREEDOM**

The band walked off stage in Tokyo to deafening applause, having blasted their Japanese fanbase with the riotous techno ending to 'Mountain People'. Gruff stepped through to the backstage area and, after towelling his newly shorn hair, flipped open his rubbery new mobile phone to text the tour manager. All of a sudden a tingling breeze seemed to float through the room, and the neon lights above began to flicker. Sensing weirdness in the room, Gruff turned to find a short Japanese girl standing in front of him, her face illuminated by UV eyeliner, but shadowed by a floppy hat.

'The bear on your album cover . . .' she whispered discreetly. 'It is the incarnation of a Shinto god, from ancient times. It gives you good things but . . .' She turned and looked over her shoulder. 'It also brings you problems.'

Gruff nodded. 'Yeah!'

The girl whispered again. 'Look for Susanoo-no-Mikoto, the God of storms as well as sea magic. I go now.' As she left the room the lights flickered back on again, and as Gruff stood there scratching his head, the other Furries began to arrive.

*

Meanwhile back in London, Alan McGee was buzzing Brian Cannon into his office to discuss the music video for 'Demons'. Cannon had directed every video for the Furries so far with his usual flair, but this time he had a radical new idea to propose.

'Let's go to fucking Colombia.'

'*That's* your pitch? "Let's go to fucking Colombia"?' laughed McGee, though Cannon could see there was a twinkle in his boss's eye. 'Jesus Christ, as soon as the band hear that idea, they're going to go for it like a shot.'

Brian explained that he knew Andrew Loog Oldham, the legendary Rolling Stones manager, who was now living out in Colombia with his celebrity wife, a glamorous South American actress. The plan was simple: Oldham would meet them for two days in the jungle before taking them up the mountains to the capital city of Bogotá. McGee rolled the idea around in his head for a minute, than rang Creation's video production manager. 'Look into the options and get back to me,' he murmured.

Half an hour later, the production manager strode into the office with an air of officialdom.

'It's a "no", I'm afraid, Brian. Colombia's off. Civil war has broken out over there, it'd be far too dangerous to go.'

Brian stood up. '*What?* Are you taking the piss?'

'It's civil war, Brian. They're simply not having it.'

An hour later, Cannon sprang into action, convinced that the video production manager was being needlessly obstructive. After making a few calls, to his surprise he found himself being connected to the British Embassy in Colombia.

Over in Bogotá, the ambassador sat bored at his desk, toying with a snow globe. The phone rang.

'Hello, the British ambassador speaking,' he piped up in a precise, BBC accent.

'It's reception, señor. There is a creative director on the phone from England. He says he wants to speak with you about the political situation.'

'Well, I suppose you'd better put him on.'

There was a click.

'Hello, the British ambassador speaking.'

Brian immediately went into speech mode, explaining how he worked for a Sony-backed record label who wanted to shoot in Colombia. The video would be a celebration of their culture, promoting tourism and casting the country in a positive light. 'But,' he added, 'I've been told there's a civil war breaking out?'

There was a pause. 'Just a minute, Brian,' said the ambassador, putting down the receiver and leaning out the window. He paused, listened for a few seconds, then returned to the phone. 'Everything looks jolly fine to me!'

Two weeks later, the Super Furries played at Reading festival, then drove overnight to the Hilton Hotel in Holland Park, London. At 6am the next morning, they were picked up by coach to begin the journey to Colombia.

With *Radiator* climbing steadily up the charts, Alan McGee had signed off £30,000 in cash for the 'Demons' video, which was split between two briefcases, one carried by Cannon, and the second by his video producer Martin Catherall. Travelling with them were the band, an *NME* journalist, and Andrew Loog Oldham's cocaine dealer, Bob.

The coach roared off into the dawn and everything seemed to be going smoothly, yet they were barely fifteen minutes into their journey before Cannon noticed an empty bottle of rum rolling down the aisle. He looked back to see the Furries, absolutely trolleyed – and they hadn't even reached the airport yet. As Brian later noted, 'No wonder Gruff lost his passport.'

Back at Creation, Alan McGee was waking up from an all-night party. There was a gentle knock on the door from his press officer, who had brought him a cappuccino. She found him collapsed on the sofa, staring at the ceiling.

'Are you alright, Alan?' she said.

'I've just given Brian Cannon £30,000,' he muttered, 'to take the Super Furry Animals to Colombia.'

'Oh,' said the PR. 'Are you *sure* that's a good idea?'

Eight hours later, the plane touched down in Miami. The Furries had sobered up by now, yet a new problem had suddenly emerged: not only had Gruff lost his passport, but the connection flight was only an hour away. They'd have to act fast and definitely not panic.

After an initial burst of panic, Martin Catherall speedily walked the singer through to immigration control. 'Don't worry,' grinned the producer. 'If you don't get your ticket, it's me and you in Miami tonight. I've got fifteen grand!' An hour later, the plane to Bogotá took off with everyone on board. The Furries, exhausted, fell instantly asleep. Yet there was something troubling Brian. Looking around, he couldn't help but notice something curious: there were only eight people on board.

'Martin,' he said, tugging on his producer's shirt. 'There's nobody else on this plane.'

'Well, of course not,' said Catherall. 'We're flying into Bogotá!'

Brian laughed uneasily, but the more he started to think, the more he started to freak. He had no address, no contact numbers, no map indicating what to do once they landed in the jungle. The only guarantee that Oldham would even meet them had come from a cocaine dealer called Bob.

'And I'm thinking, "What the fuck have I done here?"' Cannon remembers. 'Everybody's blind drunk, I haven't got a fucking clue where I'm going, I'm flying into the most dangerous country in the world, and I haven't even got an address for when we get there.'

Brian attempted to reassure himself, reasoning that Bob knew Oldham – that Oldham was their man on the ground, that everything would be fine.

'But then,' says Cannon, 'I looked to my right to see Bob tugging on an air hostess's skirt, saying, "Alright, love, have you got any Valium?" And I thought, "Oh no!"'

Four hours later the plane began descending over the roof of the Amazonian jungle: a glowing canapé of luscious greenery, stretching over the horizon as far as the eye could see. It was beautiful, yet as the plane touched down on the runway, Brian was still gripped by a sense of doom. Then, while they waited to get off the plane, a voice came over the plane intercom: 'Señor Cannon, calling Señor Cannon. Can you please come to the front of the plane?'

Brian walked nervously down the aisle, aware that he was travelling not only with a cocaine dealer, but also with two suitcases full of cash. At the end of the plane, the cabin door swung upwards.

'Brian! So pleased you could make it!' said the British ambassador to Colombia. 'You look shagged out, old boy. Come and meet your old friend Andrew – he's waiting for you at the front of the airport.'

Andrew Loog Oldham met the party in a fleet of pick-up trucks stacked with Colombian beer, after which they began the descent from Bogotá into the jungle. At almost 9,000 feet, Bogotá is one of the world's highest-altitude capitals, yet the band were descending to 5,000 feet to the forested valley of Santandercito, where they had rented a villa.

The drive lasted for several hours as they went deeper and deeper into the jungle, the pick-up trucks eventually swerving into a clearing, with a villa at its centre. Their home for the next four days was a huge Spanish house that a colonial Englishman had painted blue and transformed into a hotel. The building was to give them a curious insight into the politics of the jungle. 'I was having a drink and a smoke out the back,' remembers Cian, 'and this guy walked past with a rifle and a cowboy hat on. I said, "What's *he* doing there?" and was told: "He's there to protect you!"'

The crew soon became accustomed to the sight of armed gunmen patrolling outside the villa. It was the militia lurking in the jungle, however, who continued to provide cause for nervousness.

'It was all very mysterious,' says Guto. 'You had this sense of a world in the shadows. You knew that in the jungle there were paramilitaries somewhere. But then, the jungle's enormous, probably the size of Wales. I was definitely out of my comfort zone.'

Whoever it was that resided in the jungle, one thing was for sure: they were definitely interested in their new guests. First of all, the mafia approached the hotel's doorstep to check who was inside, then an hour later the army appeared, and eventually the guerrillas too. The political make-up of the area was complex, to say the least.

'There were pockets of FARC, the Marxist guerrilla group, controlling areas,' says Gruff, 'and then there were areas controlled by the paramilitary groups based around the drug cartels. There was also central government, who were aligned with the paramilitary groups. And obviously a lot of areas where they interacted with each other.'

The process of the local paramilitaries investigating the Furries lasted for around a day, after which they sent a message to the hotel by fax, to deliver their verdict. Oldham ripped it off the printer and assembled everyone by the swimming pool. He read:

WE KNOW YOU HAVE GRINGOS IN THERE. BUT WE ARE COOL WITH IT. WE ARE HAPPY YOU ARE VISITING IN THE CAPACITY THAT YOU ARE.
 WELCOME TO COLOMBIA!

Reading between the lines, Oldham explained that the guerrillas had realised they weren't in town to make a documentary condemning the Colombian drug trade, but instead to shoot a pop video.

The fax came as a relief, but the group were still aware that they had to tread carefully. Brian had been warned by one of the guards that the thieves in Bogotá preferred to chop your hand off than spend time removing jewellery from your fingers. Although he suspected the integrity of this advice, Brian nonetheless spent the first evening hacking his ring off with a miniature saw. As it transpired, he needn't have bothered. 'It turned out to be a crock of shite!' he laughs today.

The crew spent their first night drinking at the villa, having imported a crate of Colombiana into the hotel in their pick-up trucks. Oldham was a gracious, wizened host, and as they sat about laughing in the spacious atrium he began to tell them stories.

'In some parts of the country, the guerrillas hold a pretty firm grip on the culture,' he explained. 'There was one incident where they stormed a local church and rounded up all the men, separating them from the women.' Everyone in the room went quiet as Oldham continued. 'Well, they lined them up against a wall and put guns to their heads. Those poor motherfuckers thought their time was well and truly up. But then the guerrillas leaned towards their ears and whispered: 'Be good to your wives.' Then they left again! It was a fucking power trip, but I tell you – those sons of bitches never cheated on their women after *that*.'

In the morning the Furries and their crew jumped into the trucks and drove towards a local village called Tena, where Oldham had promised 'something cool going down'. As the trucks sped through the jungle, Gruff could hear distant drumming and the sound of trumpets being played. They finally skidded to a stop on the edge of a mountain, and Oldham explained what was happening – or rather, what was about to happen.

'This village is governed by a Marxist mayor,' he announced to the convoy, 'and today is the sixtieth anniversary of the downfall of their local landowner. From today they celebrate with a three-day fiesta!'

The trucks skidded down the hillside, and began speeding into the heart of the region. As they tumbled forwards, Bunf shouted over the noise and turbulence to ask Oldham what had become of the local landowner.

'They chopped off his head and kicked it down the road like a football!' he shouted back.

Within the hour the band and their crew were dressed in cowboy hats, drinking Mexican firewater and acting like *banditos*. They'd rented an armed guard for twelve dollars but the locals seemed friendly enough – and anyway, they were getting so ridiculously drunk that any sense of looming danger slipped away. 'It was like Glastonbury without the fence,' says Brian Cannon now. 'You knew this was unbridled freedom; it was real.'

As night fell on the valley, Oldham began to put word around that it was time to leave. Knowing the jungle as he did, he said there was no way of guaranteeing they wouldn't get kidnapped if they stayed out after dark. Gruff and the band took a look at their security guard, conferred with each other and agreed: it was time to flee. Brian Cannon, however, was outraged. The director jumped up on the bar and launched into an impassioned speech.

'We'll never come to this village again in our lives! This is our moment! Are you going to go back to your fucking hotels and sleep? Or are you gonna fuckin' live your life and celebrate with these people?!'

Everyone looked at one another. 'I mean, what's the worst thing that can happen to us? We get killed? So what! When was the last time you went to a fiesta in the Andes? Fuck going home! Let's stay here for three days!'

Before Brian's intervention, the general consensus had been to leave. After it, they were drinking firewater till dawn. The mayor of the village introduced the band on stage to a chorus of Mexican trumpets and mountain salsa music, and all the locals appeared to turn super friendly, bringing drinks to their table voluntarily. 'It turned out later the fiesta had bribed the locals not to hassle us,' says Daf today. 'Gringos in the village normally wouldn't last two minutes. They'd strip you naked.'

# CHAPTER 12
## DEEP SLEEP EARTHQUAKE / BIG TROUBLE IN BOGOTÁ / DEATH TO THE MONARCHY

Those three days in the villa turned out to be among the most blissful and liberating the band and their crew had ever spent. On the fourth day, however, it was time to return to Bogotá, and nobody knew quite what to expect. Back in the pick-up trucks, Brian Cannon noticed an immediate change as they drove up the mountains and into the outskirts of the capital.

'We'd come from this beautiful place where it seemed to be sunny all the time and, even if you were poor, you could have grown your own food, it really wasn't that bad. But then we drove up the mountain and got to Bogotá and there's this tent city, a shanty town – and it seemed to go on for miles. I've never seen such abject poverty in my life. And you could understand why it was such a violent place, compared with the countryside.'

By the time the band got to their hotel, night had fallen again. Their producer Martin Catherall had suffered a nosebleed on the way and so handed his stained shirt in to the late-night receptionist, asking her to 'take care of it'. And, with that, everyone crashed so deeply that they slept through a small earthquake.

In the morning Martin awoke bright and early to walk down to reception. 'Hiya, love, has me shirt been laundered yet?' he asked.

The receptionist looked panicked. 'Oh, señor, we took it outside and set it on fire! We thought you were in trouble!'

Martin raised an eyebrow and walked out of the front, muttering to himself. The hotel had assumed that he'd shot someone. 'It was a barometer of the psyche of the city we were in,' says Brian Cannon.

Once everyone was up and packed, they took a walk into town to scout for filming locations, with plans to meet Andrew Loog Oldham at a Chinese restaurant for lunch. With skyscrapers nestling among huge mountains at one end, and decaying housing framing gangland at the other, Bogotá was a visibly divided city.

The Furries joined Oldham, who was at the back of the restaurant having a smoke with their hotelier. Discussion naturally turned to where they were going to film, on which point the hotelier had some stern words of advice.

'Did you see the district immediately parallel to this one?' The Furries nodded.

'That is the crack district. On no account go there!'

The glint in Brian Cannon's eye returned. 'Hang on, why on earth not?' He stood up. 'Look, we're here in Bogotá, aren't we? So let's *film what goes on* in Bogotá!'

The hotelier shook his head. 'I really would recommend that you do not go there!' he protested.

'Look,' said Brian, 'we're not just in Colombia to shoot the beauty of the countryside, we have to show what's going on in town too! Otherwise we may as well be shooting in London or Manchester or Bangor . . .'

Gruff recalls the scene. 'So Brian gives this speech and the next thing we're heading into the crack zone. It was an interesting situation. Suddenly the roads stopped being paved and old women would appear at windows making throat-slitting gestures, signalling at us not to go any further. It became apparent that it was an extremely shady district.'

It wasn't long before the shady omens turned into a dangerous reality. They came to an alley. They'd barely been there for two minutes when small stones began to zip past them – one narrowly missing Brian's camera. Determined to continue filming, Brian proceeded to shoot the band while walking backwards.

'Ignore the stoning!' he directed.

Oldham, however, took a dire view of the situation. There was no ambiguity: the signs clearly indicated that if they kept walking down this street, they would become paella.

'We have to get out of here now!' he insisted.

Suddenly a gang of pirates stepped out from a dark, fishbone alley, their leader raising his machete into the air.

'You . . . you *Americans*!' gnashed the pirate.

'We are not Americans!' announced Brian.

'You make film about drugs! In bad way you make Colombia look!'

'We make nice film about Colombia! We make pop video!' replied Brian – though even he suspected that his tactics were not working. Seeing that the machete wielder was not backing down, Oldham placed his hand on the filmmaker's shoulder.

'When I say run,' he murmured, 'run . . . RUN!'

Brian bolted, but just as they turned to sprint a police truck swerved across the road in front of them, a trio of machine guns popping up from behind its speedily opened doors. A furious argument in Spanish broke out as the Furries and their film crew were ushered away from the district by a small battalion of armed cops. The shouting wasn't being aimed at the pirates, however, but at the band. 'They gave us a hell of a row for being there,' says Gruff.

'They thought we were Yanks,' adds Daf, 'and they fucking hate Yanks.'

The Furries and Brian conceded it would be wise to adopt a lower profile from that point onwards. This, however, was easier said than done: whichever way they cut it, they were pale Europeans carrying two briefcases stuffed with cash.

It was time to unwind, so later that night they caught taxis out to the city's largest nightclub. It was a UV-glowing bunker that had modelled itself loosely on Manchester's Haçienda, playing European and American techno. As the band were guided past the red ropes of its backstreet entrance, the club's owner was already taking notes on these seemingly affluent Europeans.

'Make sure they're looked after,' he whispered to a waiter, patting him on the back.

'Si, señor, I look after the English visitors!'

'No, you imbecile!' hissed the boss. 'They're not English! They're from Wales! They're Welsh! From Wales!'

'Si, señor, from Wales.' The boss dusted off the waiter's shoulder pads and sent him out to buy their guests a round of drinks.

Inside, the Furries were already getting reacquainted with Colombiana, a local drink consisting of lager, rum and soda. Behind closed doors, however, a small crisis was developing in the kitchen. Several of the club staff were gathered around a TV, which appeared to be announcing news of a fatal car crash. The junior waiter suddenly yelped. The words on the screen read: 'THE PRINCESS OF WALES HAS DIED'.

Minutes later he was explaining the situation to his boss. 'No!' exclaimed his superior, mopping his forehead with a tissue. 'Our guests will be inconsolable. *You* must announce this terrible news to them! But . . . make sure you do it while offering them the best cocktails known to man.'

'Si, señor!' nodded the waiter.

Out on the club floor, the messenger nervously approached SFA's table. He laid down his tray of cocktails, coughed, and respectfully made the announcement.

'Your princess is dead!'

Bunf raised an eyebrow. 'What?'

'Your princess is dead!'

Daf laughed. 'I don't have a fucking princess, mate!'

'You know Diana? She die in a tunnel! Is terrible car crash.'

'Ah,' said Gruff.

The band patted the waiter on his back and thanked him for delivering this tragic news. Bunf then promptly bought a round of drinks for all the locals. A huge toast was proposed: 'Death to the monarchy!'

'The band wouldn't wish death on anybody,' remembers Brian Cannon, 'but clearly they were not only *not* English but also republicans, and simply didn't give a flying fuck.' It was decided there and then: everyone was to have a big night out in Bogotá.

# CHAPTER 13
## WILLIAM HAGUE'S LETTER / ICE HOCKEY HOOTENANNY / BRITPOP TURBULENCE / ELECTRIC HARPS

As 1998 began, Britain was basking in the afterglow of the Labour party's general election victory over the Conservatives. There was a feeling that the country would become liberal and compassionate again, after years of political sleaze and incompetence. To add to the contrast, the new and relatively young prime minister Tony Blair invited one of Britain's biggest rock stars, Noel Gallagher, into Downing Street for a party and a few glasses of champagne. The music press saw it as a Faustian moment for the Oasis guitarist, who was breaking a taboo by shaking hands with the PM, but for Blair it was a media coup, helping his party look cool and arts-friendly.

The handshake was broadcast live on TV, and watching it through subtly gnashing teeth was William Hague, the leader of the defeated Conservative party. Hague switched off the telly and summoned his special adviser.

'Tell me, Sebastian,' he quizzed suavely, 'which British rock stars do we know?'

His aide blinked. 'I'm not sure if we know any, William.'

Hague banged his fist. 'Damn it, Sebastian, we have to return musket-fire on this thing. There's a cultural war going on out there and Tony Blair is winning!'

Hague walked to the mirror and adjusted his tie. 'I'm only thirty-six, you know,' he mused. 'There must be some pop stars that I . . . wait!' He spun round. 'My wife went to school with a member of the Super Furry Animals, back in Wales. I'll invite them over for a drink, perhaps with one or two photographers in tow. Then' – he turned to the mirror again – 'then we'll see how cool Blair really is!'

On more than one occasion in the past, Gruff Rhys had entertained the idea of disappearing and becoming an outlaw in a foreign country, notably when he'd spent time in Barcelona just prior to the band's formation. He'd never come as close to actually doing it, however, as he did in the early months of 1998.

The Furries had been offered a South American tour with Echo and the Bunnymen, and with Brazil, Argentina, Chile and more on the horizon, the singer once again felt the desire to maroon himself. 'I had this feeling that I'd never come back from that tour in South America, it was so intense,' he recalls. 'I'd had such a crazy two and a half years that I was thinking, I'm gonna do this tour then just stay there – to see what's happening in my head.'

Before Gruff had the chance to disappear, though, someone else stole his turn – and his opportunity. On the eve of the South American tour the promoter went bankrupt, changed his identity and smuggled his way into the Bahamas. The band had revved themselves up for a marathon, only to be left jogging on the start line. However, the situation had at least left them with some surplus energy, as Guto confirms: 'We were feeling productive and didn't want to stop.'

They agreed to head over to London for an impromptu recording session. Just before piling into the car, there was one last thing to do in their Cardiff HQ: sort through the post. 'Fan mail, promoter requests, more fan mail,' listed Guto as he flicked through the envelopes. Then he paused.

'Bunf, you've got a letter here from William Hague.'

'Bin please, Guto,' croaked Bunf.

The next day, SFA went underground – literally, into a London bunker called Orinoco Studios – to spend the New Year whipping together the *Ice Hockey Hair* EP. Given their past experience of being portrayed as stoners by the press, the band knew that putting a track called 'Smokin'' on the record would be a provocative move. They did, however, have a get-out clause: they'd been asked to write the song by Howard Marks, who was about to host a TV special about dope and needed a soundtrack. As Guto notes today: 'Gruff doesn't even smoke.'

The band took their main sample for 'Smokin'' from the Jamaican reggae group Black Uhuru and their 1977 recording 'I Love King Selassie', then applied to it the same technique they'd used on 'The Man Don't Give a Fuck' – namely building the sample into a groove then repeating it until either euphoria or mania is achieved.

Gruff's lyrics to the song suggested a new-found proactive attitude, with the singer suggesting that he'll *'find all my answers with minimum delay'* and that the meaning of life is *'anything you like'*. Despite these sentiments, however, 'Smokin'' was bound to be interpreted as a marijuana anthem by legions of teenage fans and music critics. Perhaps anticipating the controversy, the Furries also decided to include on the EP a song called 'Let's Quit Smoking'. Although essentially an acoustic version of the Howard Marks track, it does make the concession of featuring a smoker's wheeze in its rhythm section.

By the time the band recorded 'Ice Hockey Hair', the song had already been through as many incarnations as Doctor Who.

Starting life as a simple piano melody during the *Fuzzy Logic* sessions, by 1997 it had acquired a temporary name, 'The Naff Song' (on account of the band's suspicion that its themes were cheesy). In '97 the group discovered that the Swedish slang for 'mullet' was 'Ice Hockey Hair' – and the track acquired the missing piece of its identity.

'A hell of a lot of work went into "Ice Hockey Hair",' says Guto. 'We could probably have recorded an album in the time it took to make it. We mixed it three or four times, and it ended up being quite a crazy production.'

If the Furries' music has always tended to alternate between traditionalism and radicalism, this song represents a perfect balancing of the two. Gruff's lead guitar hook owes its tone to classic seventies rock, but its sound echoes futuristically through a delay pedal. The vocal is melodic and heartfelt, but also plunged through electro filters to create a sci-fi feel. Meanwhile, the various layers of the mix are composed of Bunf's heavy guitar noise, samples and Moog synths, all blending together into a satisfying crunch.

Despite these complex ingredients, the most endearing aspect of 'Ice Hockey Hair' is that it's a touching pop song, complete with lyrics that are melancholy (*'Tell me what to do if it all falls through'*), surreally hilarious (Gruff's pre-chorus request of *'Take me to a chorus now!'*) and strangely moving (*'Now that you're here, tell me you're a non-believer'*).

By 1998, the Britpop phenomenon had reached its high-water mark, and was beginning to retract. It had served SFA well in the sense that it had created an economic powerhouse to support bands in the UK. But it had also encouraged complacency in the record industry, allowing Sony to sell the Furries abroad as the latest Britpop product; whereas the truth was actually more interesting.

'Britpop was quite a risible scene,' says Guto today. 'We didn't like the idea of flag waving and we never waved a Welsh flag – it was other people that told everyone we were Welsh.'

Nonetheless, when the inevitable reaction against Cool Britannia arrived, the Furries were embroiled. 'There was a backlash against that scene – and rightfully so – that we possibly got caught up in,' says Guto. 'I remember there being frustration about it, because in Belgium we were doing so well and getting good reviews, but [selling] so poorly.'

The *Ice Hockey Hair* EP was released in May 1998 with another classic Pete Fowler cover. This time the Japanese influences had merged with sci-fi, the cover depicting what Pete describes as 'a futuristic guy having a panic attack, possibly after smoking too much industrial skunk', superimposed over a silver backdrop.

The EP was yet again named 'Single of the Month' by the *NME*, while *Drowned in Sound* described the title song as 'the most perfect thing you'll ever set your ears upon'. Indeed, it was fast becoming apparent that SFA were one of the most critically rated bands of the era.

'I think it's because they appealed to so many different people,' says *NME*'s Alan Woodhouse of the band's rave reviews. 'Indie rockers, psych heads, techno purists and classic rock buffs could all get as much out of them as one another.

'Their quality control is extremely high, both musically and in the way they present themselves visually. I didn't start at *NME* till 2000, but by that time they were arguably the most popular band in the office.'

The verdict from music fans was no less enthusiastic. *Ice Hockey Hair* rocketed to number twelve in the UK national charts, a sign that top ten success was potentially within their grasp.

With a fresh blast of encouragement, plus some loose energy still lingering from the tour that never was, the group decided that enjoying being a band again was top of their list of priorities – and with a World Cup summer just around the corner, a demo'ing expedition to Wales was just the ticket.

The band didn't have many expectations as they pulled into a farmyard in Ewloe, North Wales, in the summer of 1998. The studio on the farm was run by a Welsh archery champion called Sandy, who by all accounts resembled an Elven hero from *The Lord of the Rings*. 'He had long blond hair and made electric harps,' recalls Guto today.

As the band arrived at the farmyard, Sandy met them to shake hands, and modestly revealed that he was dabbling in the music industry himself.

'I'm managing a great girl band, lads, they're going to be massive.'

'Ah, nice, what are they called?' asked Cian.

'Totty, they're called Totty. They're fucking gorgeous!'

The band made covert eye contact between one another and edged their way into the studio.

The goal for the sessions was simple: to lay down some third album demos aided by Michael Brennan, an engineer who the group had poached from Elastica, having identified him as a master at amplified sampling and sonic architecture. 'He was really good,' says Cian. 'If you had an idea he could get it down right away.' Even the Furries, however, had not anticipated how encouraging their new sounds would be.

'We were trying out all this new equipment that we hadn't figured out,' says Gruff, 'and we realised that we had the makings of a really progressive sound for us, sonically.'

Each member of the band had been assigned a Moog Taurus – a foot-operated analogue synth – with the exception of Bunf, who chose a Wasp synth. This led to sessions in which all the pedals were used simultaneously, the band riding their multicoloured new gear like jetskis. Similarly, each member had been given a microphone and encouraged to go sample-crazy. At one point during a tea break, Bunf slipped and crashed into his guitars, knocking over an amp in the process. By chance, Cian's microphone had not only recorded this commotion, but fed it automatically into his sampler. Listening back, the band were impressed by its weird, clanging qualities, and after Cian looped the sample Daf kicked in with a breakbeat. Suddenly the bare bones of an anthemic rhythm were in place. 'We'll keep that!' nodded the drummer, as Gruff wrote down a provisional title of 'Mobile Phone'.

This experimental approach seemed to complement the songs coming out of Gruff's head, suggesting that the radical direction of *Radiator* could be pushed even further. As Gruff explains: 'We were trying out all these weird pedals, and I'd demo'd loads of songs in Cardiff that I felt were quite strong. So we thought "Fuckin' hell, we've got a really good record!"'

It was nearly time to wind down the demo sessions and cut the album itself in the West Country. While they were in Ewloe, however, the Furries couldn't help noticing that Sandy had a mysterious business partner living out in the forest. Before leaving, they made some polite enquiries, and the secret figure's identity was revealed.

'It was Elton John's brother, living out in the forest,' recalls Gruff. 'He was like a hermit, we only saw him twice. He lived in the caravan, making electric harps.'

# CHAPTER 14
## TAEKWONDO MUSIC / LOVE LETTER TO EL NIÑO / DAS KOOLIES

With some great demos in the can and a World Cup summer round the corner, it was with a sense of revved-up energy that the band unpacked at Peter Gabriel's Real World Studios, situated in the leafy Wiltshire village of Box, in June 1998. Enormously spacious, encased in a futuristic glass-spaceship design and embedded in a lake to allow swans to float past the eyes of its musicians, it was the perfect setting for the band and Gorwel Owen to cut *Guerrilla*.

There was just one problem: Gorwel was pulling out. On the first day, he rang Gruff from Anglesey to explain that he'd been driven close to madness by a particularly gruelling session with another client.

'I just can't do it,' explained Gorwell, 'the thought of making another record right now is just too intense. I'm sorry.'

The Furries understood, agreeing to reunite with Gorwel next time round. For the immediate future, however, this presented them with a significant challenge: to produce *Guerrilla* alone.

Determined not to fluff the responsibility, Gruff vowed that he wouldn't drink during the recording process and, while in the nearby city of Bath, bought a book called *Teach Yourself Taekwondo in Seven Days*. The singer then went into exercise overdrive.

'It's actually impossible to teach yourself taekwondo in seven days,' says Gruff today. 'I had a crazy routine whereby I had to do an hour's exercise before doing taekwondo, so I was going out on the bike, doing push-ups . . . I'd never done push-ups in my life and I haven't done them since! It was fucking weird.'

Gruff suddenly started bouncing about on an endorphin high, feeding his new-found sense of rural optimism into *Guerrilla*'s spirit and practising his 'wipe on, wipe off' in the vocal booth. 'Gruff was new to exercise,' says Daf, 'so he was going bonkers.'

Unsurprisingly, the singer's lyrics began to celebrate action and proactivity: *'We should do or die'* became one rallying cry, while another song announced: *'When I get home from school I'm going to write some hooks . . . when I get home from school I'm going to write some books.'*

Gruff was clearly in overdrive, and while he'd taken a commendable stance on refraining from hedonism, the remaining Furries were at liberty to discover the wine cellar. 'It was,' says Guto with hindsight, 'a hideously expensive wine cellar.'

The recording facilities at Real World allowed the Furries to continue with the Moog-driven, sample-saturated approach they'd established in North Wales. The production was split into two studios, a huge central control room then an additional space that effectively became Cian's creative workshop, housing his samplers and techno gear. 'After each album, Cian's work station would become more and more like some sort of NASA control room,' says Bunf.

The band set up their instruments in the main live room, impressed with the huge amounts of space they suddenly had to play with. 'I had a dog at the time and one day he came to visit,' recalls Cian. 'He shat in the control room, but [the studio] was so big that no one noticed for a couple of days.'

The Furries' workload was split into a trio of activities: the morning-afternoon session, during which they would capture the physical instrument takes, the World Cup-watching session, and an evening session which would see them experiment late into the night. 'There was, as I said, a very good wine cellar too,' adds Guto.

Although Michael Brennan had been sent along by Creation to engineer the sessions, for the most part the Furries were without a referee during the recording of *Guerrilla*. 'We had to be in control, so we had to get on,' remembers Gruff. 'When you work with producers you have the luxury of arguing among yourselves. Not fighting – just having different opinions. Because it was us producing, we knew we couldn't fall out, so it was quite a happy record.'

This combination of unity, discipline and taekwondo led to some of their most adventurous music to date. One night Gruff began to play with his mobile phone, singing about the possibilities of mass international communication. Warming to the theme, Guto and Bunf manipulated the melody to the Nokia ringtone, shifting it up a key and changing two notes, while Cian brought in the sample of Bunf crashing into his gear. By the next morning the band had cut 'Wherever I Leave My Phone (That's My Home)' – on the one hand an autobiographical number about Gruff's new phone, on the other a sonic whirlwind that tapped into SFA's passion for internationalism.

One particularly summery new song suggested that Gruff had taken the advice of the mysterious Japanese girl, and discovered the Shinto god of storms. 'Northern Lites' imagines the weather system El Niño as a demanding lover – a perfect metaphor for such an explosive and unpredictable phenomenon.

'The El Niño weather system comes around from the Tropical Ocean every four-to-five years,' explains Pete Fowler. 'It's an area of warm air and sea: nature warming up naturally and causing unusual weather patterns, like tornadoes appearing in unlikely places . . . tiny fluctuations in temperature creating massive results.'

As a nod to the powers of nature, Gruff recorded his vocals in the open air outside the studio, and when it was released as a single, Pete designed a weather god to go on the sleeve.

With mobile phones and Shinto deities now informing aspects of *Guerrilla*, it was clear that Pete Fowler was inspiring the band just as they were inspiring his artwork. The two artistic entities were close to looping into one other, especially on themes such as technology and communications. 'Almost every picture of Pete's at the time contained a reference to mobile phones,' confirms Gruff, 'so I think it was Pete's influence that led to us picking up on those themes in *Guerrilla*.'

To keep themselves on their toes, the Furries formed an alternative band called Das Koolies and began jamming under this mysterious new identity. 'We had a stage in the live room where there was a Moog Taurus and a drum kit, and that's where Das Koolies formed,' explains Daf today. 'We started writing songs under that name. We started writing a Das Koolies album . . . at one point we were thinking of splitting up and starting again as Das Koolies.'

The Furries had recently noticed a tendency among bands in the Britpop scene to describe themselves as 'the best band in the world' in the press, and so decided that Das Koolies would, in a scientifically provable manner, literally be *the* best band in the world.

'We had this vision of a team of scientists sitting down and working out all the components needed to become the best band in the world,' says Gruff. 'And they'd be a band like Das Koolies . . . We made a huge variety of pie charts and graphs and came up with the perfect formula.'

In tandem with the Super Furry Animals recording of *Guerrilla*, Das Koolies recorded an instrumental album called *Steel Werks in Stone*, using a blend of Italian Botempi instruments, timpani drums and harpsichords that were lying around the studio. To complete the sense of having a parallel identity, they also gave themselves pseudonyms. 'Gruff became Al Bosnia, while the other names all had an eastern bloc, Germanic feel, because we were trying to do the Kraftwerk scientific thing, proving why a particular song was perfect with graphs and things,' says Bunf.[5]

Gruff's songwriting for *Guerrilla* contained some of his sharpest ideas to date. Yet many of the album's most radical sounds started life in Cian's sampling laboratory before being taken in unexpected directions by his bandmates: the tropical drum 'n' bass of 'The Door to This House Remains Open', the whispered party invitation of 'Check It Out', the mysterious sadness of 'Some Things Come From Nothing'. 'They were still songs,' explains Daf, 'but the way they were put together was more experimental.'

As if to illustrate this upside-down approach to record making, 'Chewing Chewing Gum' had its vocals recorded first, then a complex musical arrangement built around it. 'That song was a nightmare,' remarks Cian now, 'like trying to pour custard backwards.'

Despite being problematic to record, the origins of 'Chewing Chewing Gum' at least came from a simple place. 'My gran had told my mam not to chew in bed, 'cos it gets stuck in your hair. And I just remembered it as a funny story,' says Cian. 'It's kind of a Beach Boys thing – to have a little bit of advice, a comment on life.'

---

[5] For those hoping to hear the Das Koolies record, the odds are not good. According to their close friend Dic Ben, the difficulty factor of locating this, and the supposed lost 'rave album' the band keep locked away, is high. 'I've never come across an SFA demo tape. I personally haven't seen the rave album. I stayed for six months in Gruff's house once and went searching. Nothing. No demos.'

One decisive turn in the album's spirit came about when the band discovered some steel drums in the Real World hallway. Discreetly looking around before wheeling the drums into their own private room, the band immediately got to work introducing a calypso element to songs like 'Northern Lites'. As a result, an album that was already summery took a distinct turn for the Hawaiian.

To make matters even more upbeat, the 1998 FIFA World Cup was erupting throughout the stadiums of France, and on several nights the band drove into Bath armed with a snare drum and a French horn to catch the matches on TV. There was another reason, too, that the album was beginning to sound like a breath of fresh air: after a prolonged period of relationship strife, Gruff had become single again.

'The troubled time I was going through had been resolved by the time of *Guerrilla*,' he says now. 'It sounds corny, but I was starting a new chapter in my life. The song "Turning Tide" is about being in that moment, and my life changing, for the better – even though there is that sense that the tide's going to turn.'

Somewhere amid the thrill of making a psychedelic pop album, another development was occurring in the summer of 1998 – one that was to have a profound impact on the human species. 'It was the first time I'd clocked people looking up photos of bestiality,' Cian fondly recalls of the dawning of the internet.

This strange new phenomenon – together with its equally strange concepts, like 'forum' and 'email' and 'search engine' – was combining with the rise of the mobile phone to create nothing less than a revolution in human interaction, though for most people at the time it might have felt little more than a subtly liberating change in the wind.

This was a challenging and exciting time for the authors of 'International Language of Screaming', the Welsh speakers who'd been warned that mass communication equated to political rebellion. Suddenly the world was waking up to new networks, and the possibilities seemed endless. For Gruff, though, this revolution inspired memories of an earlier time; a time when, as a teenager, he'd similarly connected with distant voices over an invisible network. He began writing about his days as a CB radio bandit.

> *Tried my hand at the citizens band*
> *I'm a breaker that breaks*
> *And my handle is Goblin*
> *I'm on air and I'm breaking the law*
> *I just switch myself on*
> *And ten-four for a copy*

'Citizen's Band' is one of SFA's most euphoric pop songs, and with its climactic chant of 'So many ways to communicate!' it hoisted CB up as a perfect metaphor for the mobile phone revolution.

Appropriately, given the song's theme, Gruff sprinkled the lyrics to 'Citizen's Band' with the coded language his teenage CB comrades had invented to protect themselves from cops. For example, 'bear' means 'policeman', while to 'eyeball' means to meet in person. Taking this sense of encryption one step further, SFA sequenced 'Citizen's Band' as a secret track that could only be accessed by rewinding *Guerrilla* from the start *backwards*. Finally, to rubber-stamp its secret nature, they hid a glossary of the song's lyrics on the inside of *Guerrilla*'s slipcase – readable only by destroying the cardboard sleeve. The collective result was that the album became like a computer game, that users would play for months before unlocking hidden meanings.

On the final day of recording, Creation's Dick Green arrived at the studio for a playback of the unmixed album. At the time

*Guerrilla* was wild and untamed, and as Green sat slowly stroking his chin, the band had no idea what was going through his mind. The label had, after all, spent nearly £50,000 on this escapade.

'Jesus,' he muttered to nervous glances. 'Oh Jesus.' More nervous glances followed. Then he suddenly laughed. 'This record will be massive . . . and the fame will ruin you!' He then taunted the band that surely the Furries didn't *want* to become enormous.

'We'll be the judge of that!' quipped Cian.

Nine weeks and twenty-five songs later, SFA had recorded their most experimental pop album to date. On the final night at Real World, the band switched the studio lights off and left to begin the mixing phase. Yet as they did so, they cast into the shadows a pile of tapes at the back of the room that had somehow passed unnoticed. The tapes lay there in the darkness, silent, patient – waiting to be discovered by the studio's next inhabitants. On the label, a phrase written in marker pen: *Steel Werks in Stone*.

# CHAPTER 15
## PLACID CASUAL, ACID CASUALS / BEAR IN A VICE / GODS AND MONSTERS

Something was up in Café Calcio, the coolest meeting point in Cardiff. No more a café than it was a nightclub, a barbecue or an arts laboratory, the small venue with a tropical feel had begun to attract SFA and their allies, all going undercover to talk shop. 'It brought everyone together like some sort of social club,' says Pete Fowler today. 'Everyone would sit about making plans.'

In the heatwave of 1998, the Furries had some big ideas up their sleeves. Every other night Cian could be found DJ'ing at the bar with his friend Llŷr Ifans, the brother of Rhys. They'd already been dabbling with techno records for a few years under the name Acid Casuals, but one night as they sat intoxicated at Café Calcio, they conspired to expand their project into a far-reaching organisation. Within a month they opened a shop to distribute the latest sounds from Cardiff's fast-moving techno scene, and began branching out into producing new dance artists and even selling their own branded clothes.

Meanwhile, SFA decided to start a record label. The name Acid Casuals was already taken, so they opted instead for Placid Casual[6]

[6] The names Acid Casual and Placid Casual share the same unusual lineage: they were both, at various times, pseudonyms for Gruff when he was a young illustrator.

– and laid out their manifesto: 'Placid Casual retains an amateur status and an A&R policy of blatant nepotism,' they announced. 'We exist to expose the world (when we can be bothered) to songs that come our way that may be ignored otherwise.'

Witnessing the birth of both of these projects was Mark James, a Cardiff-based graphic designer who would eventually partner with Pete Fowler in designing SFA's record sleeves. 'Café Calcio was a legendary hangout,' he says today. 'One day I was there creating t-shirts and packaging for Acid Casuals, the next Gruff asked me to do the artwork for the debut seven-inch[7] on Placid Casual.'

The first major release on Placid Casual was a collection of 'songs that may be ignored otherwise' by lower-key artists, titled *Depressed Celts*. An autumnal and vibrant mix of music, the record came with a unique bonus: its cardboard packaging could be unfolded and reassembled into a 3D model of an armchair, itself the Placid Casual logo.

Super Furry Animals had created two record labels and one new album in a matter of months – and they still weren't done with 1998.

With *Guerrilla* not scheduled for release until the following summer, the band decided to drop a winter surprise in the form of *Out Spaced*, a B-sides and rarities collection. On the one hand a chance to assemble tracks such as 'Smokin'' and 'The Man Don't Give a Fuck' into one place, the record was also an opportunity to sculpt a parallel-universe album with its own unique narrative.

'None of the songs were made to be B-sides,' explains Daf. 'It's more that we try to design our albums in a sense, so they're coherent. Sometimes a bunch of songs fit into that [but] we can't

---

[7] 'Just Another Fun Love Song' by Psycho VII.

always agree.' As a result, *Out Spaced* transpired to be at the least an equal to the band's discography to date; Bunf has even called it his favourite Furries LP.

The record certainly dips into the breadth of their range, with the blissed-out techno of 'Dim Brys dim Chwys' mingling with the bonkers punk assault of 'Guacamole'. Arguably displaying this dexterity at its most impressive is 'Arnofio/Glô in the Dark', a track that flicks between hallucinogenic comedown and crunchy space-pop in the blink of an eye.

If the music of *Out Spaced* was compelling, its packaging was expertly designed to keep pace. To date Pete Fowler had already experimented with the physical shape of SFA records, with the cassette singles from *Radiator* appearing in cardboard slipcases.

Taking things a step further, in early 1998 Pete proposed the idea of an edible record sleeve to Creation, showing them research into rice paper packaging. Creation didn't take the bait, but with *Out Spaced* the artist finally got his chance to get radical. 'When we released it, someone described the result as a novelty CD cover with a nipple,' he says. 'I was like "Whaaat?!"'

The 'CD cover with a nipple' was, in fact, a rubber case that had been designed to withstand space travel, although it depends who you talk to. 'The brief we gave the designer,' insists Daf, 'was that the CD case should be able to survive re-entry into the Earth's atmosphere from outer space.'

The band eventually brokered a deal with a rubber and inflatables company, resulting in a super-thick condom-style design. The only problem was that, when it was released, many fans didn't know how to release the CD from its rubbery jaws. In fact, the answer was quite simple. 'You pinch the nipple and the CD slips out really easily,' explains Pete. 'It's quite a clever lock-in thing.'

Providing the central image for the record's artwork is another of Pete's endearing characters, this time a dazed-looking bear whose head is stuck in a vice. 'The original idea was just to take quite a cute, Nookie-style bear and put a G-clamp on his head,' he says. 'I always thought he was doing it to himself, as some sort of pleasurable thing. Maybe he's gone mad or he's just trying to crank it up to see what happens. It was just a playful idea . . . a playful idea about sadomasochism.'

Energised by the rubbery, space-proof design of *Out Spaced*, Pete set to work on SFA's next record, *Guerrilla*. There had already been some initial design work while the band were still recording the album; Fowler would pick up early demos from Creation and live with them for a while, absorbing new visions of themes that he'd partly inspired.

The album title itself suggested that the paramilitary atmosphere of Colombia had stayed with the band long after they'd returned to the UK. Naturally, SFA had no illusions of being revolutionaries themselves – by their own admission they were simply a psychedelic rock-pop band whose lives were obviously not in danger – and yet they'd remembered the 'non-violent, direct action' slogan endorsed by the Welsh Language Society, and weren't beyond using the themes they'd absorbed in the jungle as inspiration. 'And besides,' Guto says today, 'there's something about the cigars and the army shirts . . . they make for good graphics!'

Pete had, however, already depicted Cuban revolutionaries in the artwork to *Radiator*, so for its successor he set his sights on characters of a more surreal nature. He began by experimenting with 3D figures using Fimo hobby clay and paint. 'I did some fantastic work building wire frame and 3D models,' says Pete now, 'then merging those with photographic backgrounds. One of the record's themes was a big interest in technology, not just music technology but also things that seep into our life – so I wanted to bring some computer graphics into my work, 3D wire-framed things to reflect that fascination.'

Inspired by Gruff's enthusiasm for Shinto gods, Pete set about creating his own series of unique god characters for *Guerrilla*. For the cover he designed a Cyclops-style alien with octopus legs, a pipe in its mouth, a commando ammo belt and a mobile phone embedded in his forehead. 'It's quite an abstract take on the idea of a deity,' says Pete, with some understatement. 'Again it came out of the whole communications thing, so perhaps it's the god of mobile phones? It's only afterwards you really think about it, but I like the vagaries.'

Referencing the monster's inbuilt technology as well as the fact that it appears on the sleeve inhabiting the control room of a nuclear reactor, SFA suggested to *Select* magazine that it was operating the 'control panel of the universe'. Pete says of the *Guerrilla* monster's duties: 'It's a super responsible job, a super dangerous job – but at the same time quite a boring job. Making sure the meter's not going into the red and so on.' [8]

Having settled on the 3D model approach, Pete designed additional creatures for each of the record's singles. The first of these was a weather god based upon the El Niño storm system, for the cover of 'Northern Lites'.

'That song is almost like a love letter to El Niño,' says Pete, 'so I thought I'd have this weather god carrying a thermostat, with a hot and cold meter round his neck. "I am the weather, it's up to me: you're gonna go a couple of degrees warmer, see what happens . . ." So I was just trying to personify something that is a natural force. It can't be malevolent or benevolent – it just is what it is.'

Another character was inspired by the film *Holy Mountain*, in

[8] The mobile monster's nuclear location also indicates that the band had clocked the emerging paranoia around cellphone use. 'Mobile phones are supposed to cause brain cancer,' Gruff told one journalist, 'so if you smoke and use a mobile phone at the same time . . . it means you're hard.'

which the protagonist is seen constructing a series of 'rock and roll weapons', effectively guitars that double up as machine guns. Fowler gave a similar guitar-gun to his character for the 'Do Or Die' sleeve: a shady, well-built assassin navigating his way through a hall of mirrors. Perhaps unsurprisingly, his red guitar-gun also has a mobile phone assimilated into it.

Finally, a more literal approach was taken for the 'Fire in My Heart' character, with Pete designing a one-eyed creature with blue fire bursting out of his breast pocket. Although the single is effectively a straightforward love song, Pete's instinct was to hone a surreal interpretation. 'I wasn't terribly interested in [depicting] the love song-heartbreak aspect, but wanted something a little more abstract with a little link in there,' he says.

A red-haired girl with mutant antennae completed the series of gods, guerrillas and aliens, and the way was now open to see how they could manifest themselves in reality.

When *Guerrilla* was finally released in June 1999, the *NME* awarded 9/10 to what they described as a 'masterpiece', while *Pitchfork* later reached a similar conclusion, giving it 8.9/10. The consensus was in: this was one hyperdelic pop record. 'In a way we're a very conventional band – we play guitars and write a lot of songs which are not particularly of a radical template,' says Gruff, 'but sometimes we do reach conclusions which go beyond that – and we think . . . "*What is it!?*"'

# CHAPTER 16
### KAMIKAZE AT GLASTONBURY / BOUNCY GHETTO BLASTER / MASH IT UP / CREATION GOES DOWN

A cool breeze caught a lift on the warmth of the sun as SFA emerged onto the Glastonbury stage, met by the sight of thousands of people standing up in a giant wave to greet them.

With no fanfare or time to waste, the canned beat of 'Wherever I Leave My Phone (That's My Home)' began booming out, surfing the festival wind as Gruff crouched at the front of the stage to begin his unconventional rap.

> *I got mobile phone!*
> *I got mobile phone!*
> *Wherever I leave my phone, that's my home!*
> *I got mobile phone!*

Despite the album having been out for less than a month, the steel drums and ice-cool melodies of *Guerrilla* had landed in the middle of a heat wave, syncing the band with a summery audience of music fans. By the time they arrived at Worthy Farm – coincidentally a few miles from Real World Studios – the Furries were firing on all cannons. The music seemed to chime perfectly with the festival's sense of wonder, particularly on the existential melodicism of 'Some Things Come From Nothing'. Meanwhile,

Pete Fowler had figured out how to bring his aliens to life: during 'Northern Lites' an army of costumed beings joined the band on stage.

'I used to hate watching groups at festivals with a hired brass section, who usually looked bored and nothing to do with the band,' says Gruff. 'So we asked Pete to design a few costumes for the brass players. I think he made a costume based on fire, one based on one of the characters from the "Northern Lites" cover . . . and there was some kind of snow monster too.'

Among the volunteers who'd happily climbed into monster suits for Glastonbury were members of the Scottish post-rock group Mogwai. Once out there, however, the band realised that being trapped in a monster outfit was not entirely compatible with tripping on ecstasy, which they had dropped beforehand. To their relief a festival volunteer began running between them with a hamster-style water bottle, ensuring nobody collapsed.

As instructed by the band before the show, the aliens resisted the temptation to boogie and instead stood there staring outwards at the crowds, gradually raising their arms to a salute towards the end of the song.

> *Don't worry me*
> *Or hurry me*
> *Blow me far away*
> *To the Northern Lites!*

The band had also found time to embellish their back catalogue. 'The Man Don't Give a Fuck', in particular, had been revamped with a techno ending that was fluid, funky and dynamic enough to get people dancing as the show morphed into a twenty-minute rave before their eyes.

'It was a buzz,' says Cian. 'You'd get to try ideas out and see people's reactions. Some people loved it, although some people didn't get it at all and were like, "Where have all the guitars gone?"'

The band were just launching into this new version of the song when they spotted something weird at the back of the field: a van, driving slowly but surely, *into* the audience. 'He was probably just trying to go from A to B,' says Guto, 'but travelling down a very strange route. He must have been tripping, he literally started to progress very slowly towards the mosh pit.'

'I did a double take,' says Cian. 'Because you can't drive cars onto the site unless you're security, and even then they usually drive round the back, over sanctioned roads.

'So at first I thought "What the fuck is that?", but then when we realised he was actually *through* the crowd . . . that was when we thought "Fucking hell – he must be off his head!"'

At first the audience were dancing around the van and letting it filter through. But suddenly the chorus of 'The Man Don't Give a Fuck' kicked in and a different crowd psychology began to emerge: people started climbing on top of it. 'It was amazing timing,' remarks Guto. 'He reached the centre of the mosh pit right as the chorus went off. You couldn't have timed it any better.'

The driver, seemingly unaware that he was parked in front of the main stage of the biggest music festival in Europe, began shaking his fist and shouting 'Get off my van!'

The next thing the band knew, the van driver was up on the roof too – and wrestling with his invaders. 'He got up there and started pushing everyone off!' says Cian. Somewhat appropriately, by the time the song had ended there was only one person remaining on top of the van – its driver. Happy. Victorious. Probably tripping.

The *Guerrilla* tour saw the band at the peak of their powers, and by now they'd learned the tricks of the road too; whenever they were scheduled to perform at student unions, for example, Bunf would feign chronic diarrhoea to get the band out of it. Meanwhile Guto had taken to studying reptiles in order to cope with travelling. 'You learn to live like a lizard and slow your heartbeat down,' he says, 'so you peak at show time.'

Although they already had the alien costumes to spruce up the live shows, the band were also deep in talks with Pete Fowler about how to make a larger statement – one that would continue the tradition of the tank and the fifty-foot bears. The solution was construed as a cross-pollination of the two, and the ultimate festival toy: a forty-foot inflatable tape deck with a cassette door that lowers to reveal a DJ booth.

'It was intended for Glastonbury as somewhere to hang out, have a smoke, put some records on,' says Guto. 'Basically it was conceived as a giant sculpture; a PA and turntables boxed together until it looked like an eighties ghetto blaster.'

The band phoned up Creation to book John Andrews for one of his pub meetings. This time, though, Andrews was on holiday in Hawaii – so it was agreed to put the bouncy ghetto blaster on hold until their fourth Creation album, and concentrate on their next show.

Mash Up the CIA was the name affixed to the band's biggest gig to date; a takeover of the 6,000-capacity Cardiff International Arena, with Howard Marks and a Massive Attack DJ set booked in as support. The question, as usual, wasn't 'how could it be done?' so much as 'how could it be done radically?'

'We were totally inspired by the KLF, and this idea of "funkadelic": loads of people on stage, total chaos,' says Guto. 'The KLF's ideas and attitude really challenged the norms, and I think possibly we were a bit like them, in that we found ourselves having access to funding for ideas. Their reactionary side was very cool, but the show they put on was the biggest thing for us.'

The Furries decided to make Mash Up the CIA their first

concert in surround sound, with a six-speaker stack suspended from the venue's ceiling and seven monologue points positioned in a hexagon shape around the outer ring. In some ways it was a recreation of the festival wind phenomenon that Gruff had noticed at Glastonbury, but one that could be orchestrated. 'It would have been like walking into a club with sounds flying around everywhere, and everyone getting the same vibe – whereby people at the back would have the same buzz, sonically, as people at the front,' says Cian, who controlled the surround. 'The sound guy had worked out the practicalities of it all, so I just had to decide which elements to send him in surround. I had six outputs instead of just the stereo, so I could feed him independent tracks.'

The band grabbed the reins of this new technology and broadcast their most conceptual show to date live on the BBC, with saluting aliens, mariachi trumpet players and a horn section dressed in mystical robes. To cap it all off, a distant relation of El Niño blew an ice storm in through the venue's open doors.

As the *Guerrilla* tour rolled into Spain, the band were introduced to Dr Kiko, a mysterious Italian pharmacist. Wild and shaggy-haired, yet highly educated – he had a PhD – and considerate, the good Doctor also had unlimited access to pharmaceutical drugs. Yet, far from being the Furries' dealer, he emerged into their lives as a simple merry prankster who they clocked as being like-minded – and invited on the road.

'My grandfather was a pharmacist. My father was a pharmacist. I was running a pharmacy with my brother in Italy before I came to Britain,' says Dr Kiko of his family tradition. 'Pharmacists are actually more mental than musicians. I went to a Pharmacists with Addictions meeting once . . . the pharmacists are crazy and mental.'

Perhaps as a result, Dr Kiko came to abandon the hedonistic

world of medicine, and become a rock tour manager instead – swearing off drugs soon after.

Although he never came to work with the SFA professionally, it wouldn't have been strange if he had: by 1999 the band had established a working network that consisted almost entirely of their friends and neighbours.

This manifested itself from the top down: the band's manager until 2009, Alun Llwyd, was an Ankst Records original. Gruff's neighbour in Bethesda, Les Morrison, became their guitar technician. They even employed staff from Café Calcio as on-tour caterers. 'Our whole point as a band almost was to bring our friends and contemporaries with us on this strange journey,' says Gruff, 'and not get swallowed up by the music industry machine.'

One other friend who joined the ride was Karen Holzbaur, who'd been running a hugely successful online fan community for the group from the States. After bumping into her at a show in New Jersey, Guto clocked her as 'that internet lady', and SFA's multimedia adviser Rob Giles promptly gave her the job of online editor for superfurry.com. 'I updated the news on the site from over the ocean for about three years,' says Karen. 'I rarely heard from anyone from management or the label – instead I mostly gathered up what I found and shared it remotely, with my website login. It worked . . . sort of!'

Later that summer, Gruff's father Ioan passed away. The Furries duly cancelled a series of shows, yet the sense that they were living through strange times lingered: corporations began to circle them like vultures, offering vast amounts of cash in exchange for advert soundtracks. Levi's placed thousands on the table for 'Night Vision'. The Labour party invited them to play an oil-sponsored show for the Welsh Assembly, to the tune of £60,000. The band turned them all down: they had grown up in such a politicised environment that, although it seemed absurd to refuse such money, they couldn't stand to mingle with politicians or corporations. When they later signed a record deal with Sony, the whiff of double standards was not entirely lost on them.

'In terms of ideology we're extremely contradictory because, you know on the one hand we were signed to Sony and on the other we were turning down advertisements from various corporations,' says Gruff. 'But we're happy to acknowledge the absurdity of our situation. We find the whole rock and roll world extremely absurd and I think we wanted to point that out by being . . . as absurd as possible.' Besides, as Daf puts it today: 'Sony owned 50 per cent of Creation all along, anyway.'

Right now something far harder to live with, however, was about to hit them square in the jaw. Midway through a soundcheck in Gothenburg, the band spotted Mark Bowen at the back of the hall. They jumped down to meet the man who had once signed them to Creation Records, only to notice a solemn look on his face.

'There's good news and bad news, folks,' said Bowen. 'The bad news is that Creation is coming to an end.'

Eyebrows were raised. 'Holy shit! What's the good news?'

'The good news,' said Bowen, 'is that I still have the company credit card!'

After the show everyone hit the bars, relieved to let their hair down in a city where booze was crazily expensive. Once piled back into the hotel room, the band commemorated the night Creation croaked by writing the song 'A Frosty Night in Gothenburg', a doom-laden spoof of the summery Dodgy song 'Good Enough'. Among its lyrics:

> *If it's bad enough for me*
> *It's bad enough for you*

*If it's bad enough for two*
*It's bad enough for three hundred.*

Despite their attempt at gallows humour, the future of the band was uncertain indeed. Gruff had already begun to demo an enticing collection of songs in Welsh – but what was to become of them? On the surface of things, the fourth SFA album seemed unlikely to survive; yet a similarly unlikely solution was about to walk through the door.

'The distributors were like "Give it to us! We'll put it out for nothing!"' recalls Bunf. 'All the people you needed to get the record on shelves were up for it, so all we needed was a label – and we already owned one.'

It was time to cut a deal. The band agreed to buy their forthcoming album off Creation Records for £6,000. For this money, they would take the chance of releasing it on their own label, Placid Casual, and recoup whatever royalties came their way. It was time to part ways with the label that had made their name, and start flying solo.

'And that was the last great Creation band,' says Alan McGee today. 'They were the last really great signing. There are only a few bands you could make a film out of, and SFA are one, because their story is so fucking bonkers.'

# CHAPTER 17
## RECOVERED HISTORIES / THE ROMAN ROAD / SMOKING GOATS / POP STRIKE / AMERICA

There is an ancient Welsh belief that anybody who makes music in the native language will be possessed by demons. Not just any old demons, however: specifically the type that make you competitive with, and jealous of, other musicians – hence the phrase 'cythraul canu', which means 'devil singer'.

As the turn of the millennium loomed, it was this myth that was preying on the minds of the Super Furries who, after four LPs, were finally getting round to recording an album in their first language. *Mwng* would prove to be their most enigmatic record, their most timeless and also their most raw. And as many of these things tend to do, it started with a simple idea.

'We'd decided to make an album in ten days,' says Guto. '*Guerrilla* had taken a while, which wasn't a problem at all, but we just felt like doing the opposite.' As usual, there was a bit of bouncing-off-the-last-record going on. However, it wouldn't be the spontaneous recording alone that would differentiate *Mwng* so dramatically from its sunny predecessor.

Many disparate fragments came together on the album with almost spooky timing, but it was Gruff's demos that provided an important launch pad. Following his father's death, he had returned to Bethesda to be near his family. One especially rainy day, Gruff climbed up into his parents' attic and found a box full of records from his formative years.

Back in his teenage bedroom, he sat on the bed listening to bands such as the 1980s new wave Welsh rockers Datblygu, as well as the folk-rock albums of Meic Stevens that had soundtracked his childhood. Inspired, Gruff started to use the wet weekends as an opportunity to visit Gorwel's studio on Anglesey. He began to demo a series of Welsh-language songs that felt like the winter to *Guerrilla*'s summer: songs of identity crisis, globalisation, war, loss and heartbreak – as well as a few melodic pop tunes too, naturally.

'My four-track recorder had been stolen,' remembers Gruff, 'so I started going up to Gorwel's for a day at a time – for social reasons, or at least that was the idea – and I'd throw down twenty songs. It was really basic stuff, sometimes to a drum machine, just a case of getting the song down.'

These demos formed the basis of *Mwng*, yet they were far from constituting the album itself. That would happen the following month when the band joined Gruff up in Anglesey, and – as ever – ideas were soon flowing between them all.

'The relationship we have as musicians is a very close one,' says Gruff, 'so I never felt the need to tell anyone what to play, or anything like that. We're not talkers – once the song is explained everyone just jumps in – and I think around that time we'd just play those songs out and everyone would help arrange them and craft them.'

In some ways, the decision to make *Mwng* a Welsh-language album was circumstantial: the band had never translated English songs into Welsh or vice versa, and, simply put, had now found themselves at a place where they had enough Welsh songs to make a record.

'The songs existed anyway and Welsh is the language we speak with each other, so in that sense it wasn't a big deal,' says Gruff. 'But in reality it *was* a big deal because we'd gone through quite a turbulent time of hype and TV documentaries where people followed us round the country with a stopwatch measuring the percentage of songs we sang in English.'

The Furries were certainly aware that recording their first album in their first language could be interpreted as a patriotic statement. The National Assembly for Wales had recently been established, devolving Welsh government from Westminster and stirring a sense of national pride. For better or worse, the Furries were aware that *Mwng* could be interpreted as a statement of some sort.

'People were passing early day motions in parliament and things like that – and ultimately we're a band of musicians touring nightclubs, you know? So maybe we didn't want that kind of responsibility,' says Gruff.

Instead, they sidestepped the political scene by touring *Mwng* in America – and leaving England and Wales to their own devices.

'We were aware that if you did a gig in Wales it could just turn into a big Welsh gangbang,' says Guto. 'It's weird, though, the Welsh thing – because we are fiercely proud of being Welsh. It's just that fine line between being proud and being a dickhead. We're not anti anyone else, there are no superiority complexes.'

Despite the band's decision to avoid any patriotic undertones, the songs Gruff had written for *Mwng* couldn't help but express solidarity with – and hope for – the language he loved, as well as numerous references to Welsh folklore and pop music.

In the past, SFA had written jokingly about the fragility of Welsh as a minority language: around the time of *Fuzzy Logic* they had written a song called '(Nid) Hon Yw'r Gân Sy'n Mynd i Achub Yr Iaith', which translates as 'This Is (Not) the Song That Will Save the Language'. Yet even this song contained some more sensitive analysis, as Gorwell explains. 'In the song, Gruff refers to "dim ond carreg mewn wal barhaus", which describes the music as being a stone in a continuous wall. And I think what the band created on *Mwng* was quite a significant stone in any wall.'

In 1999, new census figures were released showing that Welsh speaking was in decline. Gruff addressed the problem in the song 'Pan Ddaw'r Wawr'[9] expanding the theme to highlight the threat that globalisation poses to all indigenous languages.

Elsewhere, in 'Sarn Helen', Gruff turns his attention to the old Roman road of that name which once connected North and South Wales, but is now an overgrown and unusable trail. Gruff uses the song as a call to revive Sarn Helen in order to make it easier to get from one end of Wales to the other – while subtly considering the implications of the two ends of the country being cut off from each other.

'Not much attention is paid to infrastructure in Wales – they shut down a lot of the railways in the sixties,' he says. 'I think it was a kind of a divide-and-rule policy where they put fast roads from North Wales to Manchester and then from South Wales to London – so there wasn't that much in the middle, whereas in the Roman times there was a pan-Wales highway.

'Having toured a lot around Wales, it takes five hours to get from North to South and there didn't used to be many petrol stations – so we'd sleep in vans halfway up! The song was like a weird infrastructure wish-list to revive Sarn Helen, from the perspective of the touring band!'

As for the myth about Welsh-language songs causing the demon of competitiveness to inhabit your soul, the band decided it was best to exorcise it – so they put it in a song.

'What the demon does is makes you hate all other musicians

---

9 'When Dawn Breaks'

and other singers,' explains Gruff, 'and that's perceived as a truism in Welsh culture. It often isn't the case with bands, who are less competitive in the traditional sense, but it was seen as a trait of people who sang in Eisteddfods and things, because in a lot of Welsh traditional singing competitions you were competing for prizes and kudos.'

The Furries confronted the demon in 'Ymaelodi Â'r Ymylon', which translates as 'Banished to the Periphery' – a sly nod to the fact that some Welsh patriots considered the Furries to be culturally exiled. 'We'd gone through a weird time in terms of the Welsh language,' says Gruff, 'whereby we'd been quite young and we kind of ditched the language in quite a dramatic fashion! Or at least we could have been perceived to do that.'

'Ymaelodi Â'r Ymylon' reflects this strange relationship with a mood swing that verges between sea-shanty optimism and psychedelic doom.

Indeed, although the overall tone of *Mwng* is colder and more desolate than previous SFA records, it isn't a record without sunny intervals. For every song that feels like the howling despair of war ('Pan Ddaw'r Wawr') there is a breezy pop song ('Dacw Hi') or a bittersweet cover version ('Y Teimlad', originally by the aforementioned Welsh new wave group Datblygu). Another pop song, 'Ysbeidiau Heulog', ended up being one of Guto's all-time favourite SFA cuts. 'It's like an old reggae record where you can hear the mute buttons being pressed on the desk,' he says. 'There's loads of phase on it, loads of cool sounds.'

In one of the lighter moments on the record, the band found time to pursue their long-standing love of wordplay. 'Drygioni' is a song about good and evil duality; but the title is also funny to Welsh speakers, because 'drygioni' is phonetically close to the English word 'drug', although it actually translates as 'mischief' or 'badness'.

Adding flesh to the ideas of *Mwng* was a band who'd been playing live virtually every other day for the past four years. This fact enabled SFA to capture accomplished recordings in their limited studio time. 'Two years earlier we couldn't have done that,' concedes Bunf.

It's arguable that Cian might have found himself at sea on a record that was, by nature, rural and acoustic. However, his contributions to *Mwng* lend a holographic tint to what might otherwise have been a more traditional record.

'There are subtle, and less subtle electronic marks on the tracks of *Mwng*,' says producer Gorwel Owen, 'though his vocal parts and more "conventional" keyboards are really important parts of many songs too.'

Elsewhere, between Bunf's middle-toned lead lines, Daf's airy and cinematic drumming and Guto's deep bass lines, what emerged was basically the sound of a band in a room. 'Everything about *Mwng* was immediate and simple,' says Gruff. 'Even the sleeve.'

Back in London, Pete Fowler was having ideas. He'd recently started collaborating with Mark James, and they were both at Pete's studio when they heard *Mwng* for the first time. Struck by its stripped-back tone, they vowed to create something that would accurately reflect it.

To begin with, Pete focused on where the record had been made, bouncing off the rural nature of Anglesey and the album title, *Mwng*, meaning 'mane'. Early ideas included a contented-looking woman riding a horse, but as the stark and almost monochrome nature of the music settled in, Pete began to develop images that were less celebratory and more brittle. Eventually, he settled on a theme.

'I liked the idea of a tough, rural creature,' he says, 'but also one that had lots of symbolism to it. Goats are evocative but also quite simple: there's the devilish aspect of a goat, then you also have phrases like "she's a tough old goat".

Meanwhile, Mark started developing a physical approach to Pete's visuals. 'The important thing for me was experimenting with the packaging,' he says. 'The decision was made to do everything black and white with white vinyl, then we came up with the idea of layers, and screen printing onto a clear sleeve.'

The result is a design of contrasts: Pete's goat skull is both supernatural and earthly, surrounded by spirit shapes yet evocative of the raw animal bones to be found on moorland walks. The image itself is simple and striking, yet Mark's packaging allows for hidden dimensions to be uncovered from beneath frosty layers of paper.

'I think we tried to approach the artwork in the same way that the band approached the music,' says Pete. 'They recorded it very simply, getting in and getting out. For us the design was quite simple too – the skull, the layered paper, the band's logo and the title. It's still probably my favourite album of theirs.'

In *Mwng*, SFA had recorded another classic album; but could they handle releasing, marketing and touring the record completely independently? Against all odds, the mood was upbeat. 'After our experience of being sold as a Britpop band,' says Guto, 'we were very aware that things can get out of control when your record is sold to other countries. Because the record was Welsh as well, we felt good about being able to control it.'

The band were also aware that, although they had hardly any money to promote *Mwng*, they were by now surfing in the slipstream of three successful records. It was a natural advantage – although they were about to be reminded that record promotion can be a chaotic art.

*

By all accounts the *NME* interview was going well: the band were sat in a cheerful Camden boozer with a writer who'd offered them dozens of 'single of the week' accolades in the past. The prospect of nabbing a front-cover feature was looking secure and the beer was flowing. Then Gruff burped out a casual remark: 'We're on pop strike,' he joked, as something of an explanation for the more serious nature of *Mwng*.

The next day the *NME* phoned. 'Well, Gruff,' they said, 'we'd like to do a photo shoot of the band holding up placards that read: "POP STRIKE!" Can you get behind that?'

'Eh,' said Gruff, 'that was really just something I said off the cuff . . . I mean, we're not really on pop strike.'

The journalist paused for a minute, then perked up again. 'No problem! How about we photograph you with empty placards, then we can just add the text later! What do you think?'

The Furries lost the cover – but quickly regained their sense of humour. The next day, they gathered together the worst quotes they could find on the album to parade in a music press advert.

'It got great reviews, but we managed to find some bad ones,' says Gruff. 'Stuff like "career suicide" from the *Jewish Chronicle*. We put the advert up in the *NME*.'

By this time, Emyr Glyn Williams of Ankst was making DVD fanzines, and on the morning that *Mwng* was released, he and Gruff wandered into Cardiff city centre together.

'We walked into HMV and there were hundreds of copies of it everywhere, like a new album by Katy Perry had come out! That's what was great: here's a record that has an audience: it doesn't matter whether it's in Japanese or Swahili: here's a band that has a following, this is their new record and people wanna buy it.'

The band's optimism was rewarded the following Sunday, when the radio announced that *Mwng* had debuted at number eleven in the UK album charts. The band were stunned by the result:

an independent album sung in a minority language was suddenly hanging out with Britney Spears and David Gray in the national top twenty. In some ways, it was symptomatic of a journey that Welsh-language pop music had undertaken during the preceding years.

'For a while in the seventies and eighties, we were communicating just with each other,' says Emyr, 'and the great thing that Ankst and these bands did – if there's anything that should be remembered or that you could feel proud about – is that there was a breaking out of that cycle, and actually making it clear that music is music. It's not just for a small audience, or a nationalistic audience, or a geographically defined audience.

'So I think that's the big change that's happened with Welsh culture: it's had to go out, and I think it's benefited a hell of a lot from doing that. And you know, there's no shame. There are lots of people who feel that using the Welsh language might be a bit old-fashioned, or not modern. But no – it's perfectly great! It's a language like any other, and for it to live and survive it has to be communicated.'

To non-Welsh speakers the mystery of *Mwng*'s lyrics may well have been part of their charm, but for those who wanted to know what they meant, mwng.co.uk was launched online. 'It was the first realisation of an album-specific site,' says Karen Holzbaur. 'It was well crafted, offering up the Welsh lyrics with English translations and even explanations.'

The morning after the chart declaration, Daf woke up on the sofa of his Cardiff flat – ruffled, croaky and with a whistle hanging out of his mouth. It had been a good night. Muttering a curse at the sunshine for getting past his curtains, he reluctantly hit the remote and started gathering empty beer cans. Then something caught his eye on the TV. It was a Welsh MP speaking in Parliament.

'I'd just like to say, well done to the Super Furry Animals for their Welsh-language chart success!' announced the MP to polite applause from the other MPs. Daf dropped the remote. 'What the fuck?'

# CHAPTER 18
## EAST COAST NEGOTIATIONS / LOST IN TIME

It was time to get away. Using the money from *Mwng*, the Furries were able to fund a tour of the east coast of the US, hopping from one state to another in a bus driven by an elderly, smiley couple they'd somehow met in Tennessee. The pair – who were just your everyday husband and wife bus-driving team – were all too happy to drive a pop group up to Boston, though their folksy ways did have a slightly bizarre air to them.

As the bus floated along the coastline of Atlantic City, business decisions were being made four hours up the road in New York. The head of Sony A&R was flipping through the CVs of Creation's bands, stroking his chin. Sony had effectively owned half of Creation, so they could now cherry-pick who to rescue from the rubble. The A&R chief stopped at the Furries' CV, muttered something to himself, and buzzed the intercom.

'Get me the Furry guys!'

The call came through from Sony an hour later, and the band requested a quick stopover at a clifftop café so everyone could make calls and discuss the offer. As a hazy sunset spread out into the sky behind them, Gruff's mobile suddenly began vibrating with an unexpected number.

'Right, you ferrets,' ranted McGee from the other side of the

Atlantic. 'What the fuck are you doing, pussyfooting over whether or not to sign to Sony, eh?'

'Er . . .'

'Who do you wanna be, the Super Furry Groundhogs? If you don't sign to Sony you're going to be touring in a van for the rest of your lives! These guys want to sign you. They want to sign you and make crazy records with you. Sign to them!'

Instead of hanging up, McGee pressed a button on his phone and suddenly Rob Stringer – one of the most powerful record company men on Earth – was on the line. Within a minute, they'd all arranged to meet in New York.

As the band continued the low-key *Mwng* tour through New Jersey, there were various discussions about how to handle things with Stringer. He was a businessman. A professional. Clearly, now was the time for dignified negotiations.

The next lunchtime, they were buzzed into Stringer's office. Immediately the signs were good. 'Guys,' he said, getting up to greet them, 'everything you've heard is true. I really want to sign the band!'

Daf's eyebrow instinctively raised itself. 'We do have some requests,' he said.

'Go for it!' said Stringer.

'Well.' Daf took a deep breath. 'We want to make an epic conceptual record with a film for every song, released on an interactive DVD in 5.1 surround sound with cinema mix options and a double-gatefold remixes edition.'

The rest of the band looked nervously at Daf.

'Oh yeah,' he added. 'And we also want Paul McCartney to cameo.'

The band looked nervously back at Stringer, who stroked his chin. Then he smiled.

'That sounds great!'

It was probably for the best that the band had decided against mentioning their other plan – the one about turning an aircraft carrier into a mobile nightclub called SFA Island. They signed the deal with Stringer, then returned to the elderly bus-driving couple who were parked outside. America was working out pretty good.

One month later, a lorry reversed into the car park of Sony's NYC headquarters. A few men in white overalls jumped out, and then pulled up its loading-bay shutters with a huge crash. After rustling about in its cargo, they started wheeling several crates out, sliding them down a ramp and towards the entrance of a huge, dark cellar.

One by one the crates sped through the central aisle of this bat-infested tomb, which was filled with hundreds of anonymous boxes. Once they'd reached a fair distance, they slammed the crates against one another – and applied the brakes. The workers then turned back towards the exit, high-fiving each other as a mechanical shutter began slowly sealing the room behind them. As the vertical door descended, it squashed a ray of sunlight into a beam that shot out through the super-sized basement, swooping up to the ceiling before zipping into darkness.

And there the artefacts of Creation Records sit to this day: the weird spools; the abandoned documents; the stolen paintings and the uncorked wine; the unsigned contracts, the Colombian telegrams and the Spanish ouija boards.

In the final bay, there also sits one crate that glows ever so slightly in the dark; and that is the crate marked: 'Das Koolies'.

# CHAPTER 19
## INTERMISSION /
## EXPERIMENTS WITH EARTHQUAKES /
## THE SKULL GOD /
## FURRYMANIA / YETI PSYCHOSIS

In many ways, SFA were the right band at the right time to write a psychedelic soundtrack to the rise of the mobile phone. They'd always been told that the language they spoke was a political choice, yet as Welsh speakers who'd defied nationalist opinion to sing in the most commonly used language on Earth, their passion for international hook-ups was already embedded by the time the comms revolution came calling. That they did this while introducing millions of music fans around the world to a language they'd never interacted with, is all the more impressive – but perhaps we shouldn't be too surprised. 'Communication is, on the most basic level, what art is all about,' says Emyr of Ankst Records. 'There is no other vocation for art, because it's basically useless, isn't it? It has no purpose whatsoever, and you can't quantify it at all! All it does is communicate ideas and experiences – that's all it can do. And Gruff is an artist.'

So that was the rise of the Super Furry Animals. Now what about the fall? After all, if the Roman Empire, the Third Reich and Ziggy Stardust have taught us anything, it's that we always get a fall after a rise. Right?

'Actually, something weird happened with the Super Furries,' says *Artrocker* magazine's Cindy Suzuki. 'They rose, then they just sort of perched. It's not normal. But after Creation collapsed, they just carried on putting out great records.'

Indeed, the band went on to record some of the most radical albums of the 2000s: albums that spoke of global technological chaos; albums that mixed Catalan choirs with political protest; albums that featured Paul McCartney chewing celery in surround sound. As you may have noticed, however, this isn't a book called *The Rise and Perch of the Super Furry Animals*. If it was, we could be looking at extended chapters, revised editions and all sorts of madness while the band are still together. To keep things succinct without ignoring what came next then, our Furry timeline will now increase in speed by roughly 60 per cent. (Those seeking a book about the perching era may wish to slow their reading speed by approximately 60 per cent to accommodate this.)

SFA recorded their first major label album, *Rings Around the World*, in upstate New York and Metropolis Studios in Chiswick – and it was in the latter studio that the experiments with earthquakes began.

'Getting our hands on this technology . . . it was kind of hilarious,' laughs Guto. 'When you make a record in stereo and put it on the big speakers, it's pretty cool. But when you do it in surround, you're dealing with sub-bass systems as well.'

The band started watching Hollywood blockbusters to see what sub-bass systems could do. It transpired that they could do a lot. In fact, as the Furries discovered the next day, they could even cause structural tremors.

'We found this frequency that made the building [Metropolis] shake, like an earthquake,' continues Guto. 'I think it was 19Hz which made a small quake in this massive building. The whole thing vibrated. Mariah Carey was recording upstairs. We got a huge bollocking.'

The music on *Rings* would emerge bigger, grander, still pop – but also more technically sophisticated than its predecessors. Familiar themes such as global communication were distilled and mixed with an awareness of how overpowering these new technologies could be, while globalisation, apocalypse and sexual paranoia lurked in the record's periphery.

'We were left by Sony to do what the hell we wanted to, which is fantastic in some respects,' says Gruff. 'They took a risk in signing us and letting us record the albums of our dreams, you know? And really experiment with recording techniques and studios and film.'

One of the record's undisputed highlights is 'Receptacle for the Respectable', an epic, bouncy pop odyssey which came about with two songs being fused together. Notably, 'Receptacle' climaxes with a death metal outro in which Gruff bellows like the hologram of an enraged alien.

'It was a bastard to mix,' says Guto.

Rob Stringer was keen to help SFA invade the charts and become commercially triumphant, so a rebranding exercise began – with Sony bringing in hip graphic design companies and Mark James to create new artwork and logos. Pete Fowler was off cover duties, but he was happy enough: he'd been commissioned to create an animated film to go with 'Receptacle for the Respectable', with his old college friend Simon Pike.

The film they came up with draws on the imagery of classic Nintendo games, with the animation going up a 'level' every time the music shifts gears.

'I love the landscapes of Mario,' says Pete, 'the little hills, and the way that you might see a mountain with eyes on it in the far distance – I love the idea of everything being alive, and a bit weird.'

Set on an alien planet, the animation charts the daily commute of a creature as he awakes, gets up and catches the bus to work. There's just one caveat: every time he bumps into another creature or being, he is physically transformed by them – like evolution in fast forward, or a Mario-style 'power up'. It ends with our protagonist being consumed by a giant Skull God, in a sequence that happily coincides with Gruff's death metal screaming.

Pete tells the story of how the Skull God came into being. 'I used to get a bus when I first started working at my studio, and every single bus ticket I'd get I'd tear the paper to make a skull shape. I did it every time, and ended up with a box full of these skulls. You had to get the ticket, fold it in half, make the shape, tear the eyes, fold that in half . . . and it would always come out different. It made me think differently about how I drew skulls.'

Unbeknown to Pete, however, as the production of *Rings* drew to a close, there was trouble brewing with Sony. The Furries had tried to muster enthusiasm for the trendy new graphics companies that the label had brought in, but there were simply too many ideas being developed by too many artists. Ultimately they wanted a singular vision back, and ultimately they wanted Pete. With just a week to go until production deadline, Fowler got the call. He was back on the sleeve.

'I was like – fucking hell. Can do!' he says. 'So we worked the stuff from the animated video into a cover. There wasn't time to start something new and that was the only thing we had – there was no fucking about.'

The Skull God blasted out of the 'Receptacle' video and onto the sleeve, luckily creating something quite iconic in the process. And with that, *Rings Around the World* was released in the summer of 2001. A full-on multimedia experience and the first album ever to be released on CD and DVD, it was complex,[10] critically acclaimed – and nominated for the Mercury Music Prize.

That summer, the band embarked on a tour dubbed Furrymania, which would give them a chance to revolutionise the way they presented their live show.

'We realised how much material we had and wanted to play it all, really. So that's when we started doing the bingo,' says Guto. 'We had all the songs written up on small bits of paper – I think it was 124 or so of them – and we'd do a show in the afternoon with a bingo machine, and people would pick songs.

'These were small gigs full up with Furry fans, which gave us the cushion if you got a song wrong, and they often knew the lyrics better than we did. Then you'd do the rock show in the night, with surround sound – which was very exciting.'

By this time the Furries had developed live surround sound into an art form, with Cian throwing the audio around the room using a specially designed joystick. This made it hard for the band to concentrate, because they'd be hearing sounds zooming around all over the place, but by all accounts it sounded amazing. According to Guto: 'This was something we'd wanted to do for years, going back to the clubbing days when music was everywhere, you weren't necessarily focused on a stage.'

*Rings Around the World* had seen SFA emerge as fresh-faced, clean-shaven and short-haired. Naturally this couldn't last – especially considering the band's tradition of bouncing off themselves

---

10 *Rings* stayed in keeping with the band's vision of albums as computer games, which, if explored, unlock new levels. For example, there is a bonus vinyl hidden inside the packaging of the gatefold edition of the LP. Most owners simply have no idea this exists. 'There's a 7-inch hidden in the back,' confirms Mark James. 'When you open up the gatefold the 12-inch vinyl is there. If you take that vinyl out, pop it and get your hand in, there's another 7-inch vinyl down the back.'

in strange new directions. It would come as no surprise, then, that things were about to get hairier. Much hairier.

'I don't think me or Bunf have ever got over it,' says Gruff of the band's decision to spend their next album campaign dressed as yetis. 'We became the yetis in costume,' he says quietly, 'and it completely changed us.'

*Phantom Power* saw the Furries produce themselves for the first time – albeit with help from Gorwel – to create an acoustic-pop record with modest flashes of glam rock and techno. The band learned on the fly how to record their instruments, and in a bid to stop acoustics from bouncing about, started building a village of indoor tents that they could record inside. Then, they started firing the machine guns.

'"The Undefeated" is a song about war, so we wanted gun sound effects,' explains Gruff. 'Cian had bought a thousand sound-effect albums off a guy who had a studio down the corridor . . . but our Scottish engineer said, "Don't bother with that – I know a guy who can deliver an AK-47 and an Uzi!" So this guy drove down with a boot full of arms. I think he was, er, licensed.'

It was 2003 and the Iraq war was raging, despite the protest of a million or so people on the streets of London. Meanwhile, George Bush and Tony Blair had forged what appeared to be an unaccountable, two-man global police force. Under these circumstances, SFA refound their political chops, directly attacking the *'Phantom lies, on the hour'* of the complicit news media, as well as the *'fast and cheap'* oil that was perceived as the bait that lured Western forces.

The title of the record itself – *Phantom Power* – is a commonly used technical term for musicians, but under these circumstances it served as an ominous pun, alluding to the sense that dark forces were stomping around the world stage.

'I think that's what got Gruff interested in that term: is phantom power the power behind the scenes, the people pulling the strings that you don't really know about?' says Pete Fowler. 'So for the cover artwork I got into the idea of these horses being the gatekeepers of power, and put them in a mountainous environment similar to Snowdonia in North Wales.'

With an increasing sense of déjà vu, *Phantom Power* would come to be hailed by the press – in this case represented by *Q* magazine – as the band's 'best album to date', and there is some agreement among fans. Whether or not it is their best record, however, there's no doubting that it contains one of their best songs.

Part sci-fi space trip, part existentialist dilemma, 'Slow Life' became a show-opening anthem to rival 'The Man Don't Give a Fuck', with its uncanny ability to walk the tightrope between techno, prog and rock without sounding like a horrifying student experiment. According to the band, its genesis spanned several years.

'Around the time of *Mwng* I was making tea with the radio on, and this classical tune started playing,' recalls Cian. 'I thought it would fit with an idea I was working on, so I pressed record quickly and sampled it back off the cassette.' At first Cian didn't view it as Furry material, but the allure of this mysterious sample refused to go away, with Bunf and Daf adding guitars and more traditional songwriting structures.

The jam turned into a song when Gruff added lyrics that dealt with the media's representation of war and its victims. 'It's about the media sanitising famine and horrors,' he says. 'With 24-hour news, famine and war become a commodity for advertisers. My feeling is that a commercial news channel is going to do whatever they can to boost ratings and maximise advertising revenue, so they're going to portray war like some kind of superficial computer game.

'But people don't forget things: their collective memory lasts for generations, it's as old as the hills. In centuries' time the kids of Iraq will still be angry about the war – it'll leave a huge scar.'

Although *Phantom Power* has its fair share of political clout, its status as a great pop album was secured by the lead single, 'Golden Retriever', the video of which revealed the band in yeti-dress for the very first time.

'We had this idea for a video where our hair wouldn't stop growing,' says Gruff of the yeti's genesis, 'and we were friends with a guy who makes sculptures and stuff out of hair, called Peter Grey. He ran with the idea, but came up with something better – and turned us into yetis.'

Peter Grey suggested that the video should be filmed on a giant glacier in Iceland, with a huge fire burning in the middle, and the yetis worshipping it. For some reason Sony found this idea 'uninsurable', however, and the location was switched to the safe confines of a North London studio.

The band spent much of the rest of the year dressed as yetis, donning the furry costumes during live encores and bringing a distinctly shaggy dimension to 'The Man Don't Give a Fuck'. Finally, the beasts were theatrically machine-gunned down during a gig to celebrate their singles collection, *Songbook*.

'It was great – like being transformed,' says Gruff of the creatures' legacy. 'None of the band are really exhibitionists in reality, so we were able to put these clothes on and become seventies rock monsters. It drove the audience nuts.'

# CHAPTER 20
## WASTELAND GODS /
## TRAVELS IN A SPACE BUGGY /
## PIZZA TRIPPIN'

A small purple weed drifted across the South American desert plain. Above it were gas stations and road signs advertising surf destinations like 'Sunny Seville', but these were rusted and creaky – ghosts of the fifties. At its remotest edges, broken telegraph poles lined the edge of a dark forest, out of which ascended thousands of crooked villas, all looming skywards up a vast hill. And there, at the top of the starry night, were the Gods. The antlered creatures stared out across the wasteland with hollow eyes protected by sunglasses, and let out a gleaming smile. For they knew that it was good.

Then, a giant human hand appeared and placed a ten-foot blob of skunk into the forest. 'At the time you couldn't tell that a quarter of the bushes on this model were made of weed,' says Pete Fowler today. 'We thought it was funny at the time! Acrylic, plaster . . . and marijuana.'

Pete and Mark James were working on a miniature model landscape to photograph for the front cover of what transpired to be SFA's final album for Sony, *Love Kraft*. The album had been recorded in Spain and mixed in Brazil, so – logically enough – the two artists had decided to base their new universe upon the concept of 'Easter Island meets Newport'.

'We wanted to build something physical, with our hands,' says

Pete. 'It was a weird South American desert plain, sort of like a shanty town. We referenced the SFA tank by having a little model made of it, and also had billboards which referenced places Gruff had gone past on road trips – these mad roadhouses in the middle of nowhere, with outdated billboards. So we were picking up on their travels a little.'

Naturally, strange new worlds require strange new Gods, and it was Mark's suggestion of a *Wicker Man*-style wooden deity that led to him and Pete creating the strange statues that overlook *Love Kraft*'s landscape. 'They're like Easter Island . . . things, in sunglasses,' Pete laughs. 'I suppose it's old Polynesian culture meets a dodgy waste ground in South Wales.'

As you might expect, the tropical nature of *Love Kraft*'s artwork reflected the music within. After working flat-out to create two multimedia extravaganzas in a row, the band had decided that solar power was needed to recharge their batteries – so flew to Catalonia, where Beastie Boys collaborator Mario Caldato Jr met them to assist on the new record.

Although they'd recorded several upbeat pop songs for the *Love Kraft* sessions, the band opted for a mellower tone when it came down to the editing. The results capture the summer heat of Catalonia, as well as the nostalgic pangs of broken relationships; all glued together with classy string arrangements[11] and an echo of Beach Boys harmonies.

Despite the band's ever-present sentimentality detector, there's a glimmer of magic to *Love Kraft* as the band allow themselves some honest, gut-punched observations on human love. Rather like the physicist Richard Feynman marvelling at our species as 'atoms with consciousness . . . matter with curiosity', SFA look at our own 'atomic lust' with both wonder and regret.

---

11 Courtesy of Sean O'Hagan.

Though playfully subversive, it's an album that aims more for honesty than radicalism, more for quality songwriting than a reinvention of songwriting itself. 'Our albums are usually quite kaleidoscopic, jumping between tempos and instrumentation changes,' says Gruff. '*Love Kraft* was a more consistent listen, less of a pop record but maybe more of a whole experience.'

For the first time, Bunf, Daf and Cian also sang lead vocals on the album, having become confident songwriters in their own right. Gruff clearly embraced the act of sharing the microphone, and today considers his bandmates' songs to be among the album's best bits. 'I love Cian's "Cabin Fever",' he says. 'That final song is really strong. I think it's a record where maybe the more quiet moments, the more laid-back moments, are the most convincing.'

Producer Mario next suggested the Furries mix *Love Kraft* in Brazil – and, after a quick spell of chin stroking, the band calculated that this would actually prove cheaper than going to London. A week later they would be sitting on a tropical beach, on the outskirts of Rio de Janeiro.

'We were working in this 1980s, *Scarface*-looking hotel on the coast,' says Gruff. 'It was out of season so it was just the five of us. Around midnight we'd finish work and go to the beach, where there was this captain who sold Cachaça, the Brazilian rum. And we'd sit there in the dark drinking rum. [*Laughs*] I think the record sounds a bit like that as well. And then we left the singles off the album, and Sony lost interest in us! But we had a great experience.'

Things were indeed heading south with Sony: the company had merged with BMG, removing the Furries' allies from the Creation era in the process. Someone new was pulling the strings – and the band sensed indifference. Luckily, they had been expecting to get dropped every day since summer 1996. So instead of being shell-shocked, they sat on the Brazilian beach drawing up plans for the *Love Kraft* tour. Serious plans. Plans that involved holographic space suits. And a moon buggy.

'We managed to get it on every stage on the tour, I think,' remembers Gruff of their lunar vehicle. 'The stage at Glasgow Barrowlands was the most problematic, because we were on the third floor of the building and we had to winch it up through a window.'

The tour also saw Gruff begin to wear a *Power Rangers* helmet on stage. The helmet, which had been discovered in a second-hand theatre prop shop in North Carolina, gave off the strange illusion that the singer's mouth was in his eyes. 'I tried a Britney Spears-style microphone, and that worked fine,' says Gruff, 'but I prefer just singing through my eye. Helmets are generally very handy for a hostile crowd . . . The threat of getting cans of lager on the head increases in a hostile crowd environment.'

In 2006, Rough Trade's Geoff Travis gave SFA a mission. Having signed them up following the end of the Sony contract, he issued specific instructions at a covert meeting: 'OK, guys,' he instructed, 'I want a classic Furry pop album.'

On the rebound from strings and ballads, this suited the band just fine – and they flew out to a studio near the French Riviera. Surrounded by vineyards and friendly wine-makers with talented feet, the *Hey Venus!* sessions took on a fruitful nature in more ways than one. What's more, the Furries were undergoing a sudden exposure to freak weather.

'We recorded in the Rhône valley,' says Gruff. 'It gets the mistral winds coming off the Alps, and it brings the icy air from the glaciers and creates a very unique icy draught even on the hottest of days – so that was the backdrop for the recording.'

A month later, they returned home to discover they'd captured an almost erratic departure from the Furry sound. Gruff again: 'I was playing songs to friends and they couldn't tell it was us, which was exciting. We realised we had a really raw, noisy record – songs like "Crazy Naked Girls" and the first versions of "Baby Ate My Eightball" – really sick songs.'

The pop mission was not forgotten, however. With one eye on honing a concise, summery album, they coaxed themselves away from the more anarchic material, and headed for the bright lights and acid-surf of *Hey Venus!*.

In the art department, things were changing fast. The Furries had made a 'blood pact' with Pete Fowler in 1997 that they wouldn't still be making records in ten years' time – a pact that had clearly run into overtime. Mutually agreeing a break, SFA looked instead to a mysterious Japanese artist called Keiichi Tanaami, who had famously been one of the first people in Japan to confess to eating acid.

'This coincided with the opening of the first pizza parlours in Tokyo,' explains Gruff. 'So he used to go into the pizza parlour and stare at all the different toppings, and get inspired and make psychedelic screen prints. So it was very interesting, er . . . getting in touch with him through lawyers and interpreters.'

*Hey Venus!* delivered on its pop mission, not least with the 'world's first secular Christmas single', 'The Gift That Keeps Giving', and the 1970s karate-chop of 'Into the Night'. Feelings about the record were more mixed than usual – with even Gruff describing one song, 'Suckers', as a failed attempt to parody generic stadium-rock balladry – but the critics appreciated the album's more direct nature, with *NME* hailing 'some of their most beautiful songs to date'.

With the resulting tour and a stage show illuminated by a huge model lighthouse, the band drew to a close an era of huge, coast-to-coast US tours. The post-Creation years had made them better known than ever in the States, yet they'd also rejected lucrative commercial offers in the name of protecting their integrity.

'We kind of spurned the financial opportunities that came our way in America,' says Gruff. 'Sprite and Coke tried to buy "Hello Sunshine" for million-dollar-plus campaigns . . . it got too weird and heavy for us. [Instead] we gave it to War on Want for free for a YouTube campaign video, detailing human rights abuses by a Cola franchise in Colombia.'

As the suitcases of cash were politely declined, it didn't escape the band that their ideals were contradictory, Utopian, possibly self-defeatist and certainly budget-zapping. Yet, for better or worse, the ideals survived – and so did their solidarity with one another. 'It's quite acceptable now for songs to be used by corporations, but the fans believed in the Furries so much, and I truly believe that the band didn't want to disappoint them,' says the band's mutual friend, Dic Ben. 'To put it simply, they're just not a bunch of cunts.'

# EPILOGUE

In 2009, I met the Super Furry Animals. *Artrocker* magazine had decided to splash the band on the cover, and having given me a mission – to capture them at work – Rough Trade laid the groundwork for me to shuttle into their Cardiff bunker, where they were recording *Dark Days/Light Years*.

The studio was located about half a mile from Cardiff Central station, down a slightly ominous back alley. Inside, there were guitars, sketchpads and strange Eastern instruments lying around on the floor. There were also strange phrases drawn on paper and stuck to the walls – phrases such as:

> WE WILL ACTIVATE THE BEAM
> THAT WELCOMES SPACE SHIPS

In the far corner of the room a video camera was resting on a turntable, whirling slowly around. Cian was sat next to it, tapping out the final details of SFA's new masterplan on his laptop.

The idea went something like this. The studio was rigged with twenty-eight video cameras. These cameras would stream the recording process live onto the web, allowing fans to edit their own film of the studio experience in real time. I told Cian that this seemed like a hugely complicated plan, but he reassured me it was 'just like running a TV station!' – which seemed to indicate he knew how to do that too.

As I sat there absorbing everything, Bunf walked into the recording room and picked up a guitar. It was time for some space noise.

'OK, hit it with the hairy muff, Bunf!' shouted producer Chris Shaw from behind his glass screen, as a massive WWWEEERRRWAAARRR blasted out from the amplifier.

Bunf was overdubbing white noise onto one of the new songs, a psychedelic stomp called 'Cardiff in the Sun'. His beard had by now grown to vast, Jesus-like proportions – something he later admitted had provoked comments from Sicilian fans.

'They point and shout "Vagabondo!" at you,' he said. 'People with beards in Italy are seen as vagabonds, although it could be just Sicily. They shout "Beaver!" too.'

A few minutes later the phone rang. It was Pete Fowler on the line, calling up to discuss the artwork he'd been working on with Keiichi Tanaami, the Japanese pop artist.

The call was placed on loudspeaker, and discussions about packaging began. Pete suggested that the CD could have a spring hidden underneath it, so when you open the case, the record shoots into your face.

'That would be amazing!' laughed Guto.

Daf raised an eyebrow. 'The record company would kill us,' he said.

After an hour of recording space guitar, Bunf finally staggered back into the mixing room, looking slightly frazzled. Everyone patted him on the back as if he was an astronaut returning from a space near-disaster.

'Let's get some takeaway!' said Guto.

A few of the Furries filtered outside, leaving Gruff and

producer Chris Shaw alone by the mixing desk. They were listening to a song that had been inspired by a recent news report from the Middle East. It stated that an Iraqi woman had arrived home one day to find that her house had been blown up by an airstrike. Everything had gone, it seemed, apart from a radio playing music from deep within the rubble. As she crouched down and listened, it became clear to her what was playing. It was Neil Diamond.

Gruff was keen that I didn't think they were trivialising her experience. 'It's just . . . sometimes you can't choose the soundtrack to your life. You know?' he said. 'A bomb can strike with the most mundane Neil Diamond song playing on the radio.

'It's not the same thing at all, but when my baby was born, the nurses put on a compilation tape featuring Dire Straits. And I was completely ecstatic! But at the same time . . .' he trailed off.

I didn't realise it at the time, but the Super Furries were to go on a prolonged hiatus following the recording of *Dark Days/Light Years*. At the time of writing, it's been about five years since an album has come out, and nobody's quite sure if they're coming back.

Time was up and my train was calling, so I took a few photos of the band, grabbed my jacket and took directions back to the station from Bunf. Before I left, there was just time to ask if he'd had a good album session.

'It's been good,' he smiled. 'We hadn't done anything in a while, so when we started rehearsing it was . . . [*adopts cheesy accent*] it was a good feeling! And you never know. Is there still life? And enough enthusiasm? And to our surprise it turned out that we still have that kind of drive. It's the only thing we really know how to do, making music. Like sitting in a comfy chair!'

I opened the door into what had become a snowy Cardiff, and

zipped up my hood. Taking one last look back into the studio, there was a phrase scribbled on the wall that caught my eye. It simply said:

*GANG OF ELK*

# SFA MIXTAPE

A selection of Furry flavours compiled by the author

1. Mrs Spector
2. Ymaelodi Â'r Ymylon
3. Slow Life
4. Citizen's Band
5. The Turning Tide
6. A Matter of Time
7. The Man Don't Give a Fuck
8. Dim Brys Dim Chwys
9. Focus Pocus/Debiel
10. Hermann Loves Pauline
11. Atomik Lust
12. Receptacle for the Respectable
13. Drygioni

14. Wherever I Leave My Phone (That's My Home)

15. Frequency

16. Guacamole

17. Down a Different River

18. Waiting to Happen

19. Calimero

20. Blerwytirhwng?

# SONG TITLE TRANSLATIONS

Rydwi'n Mynd Yn Hén
I'm getting old

Mynd Am Dro
Going for a walk

Dim Brys Dim Chwys
No rush no sweat

Blerwytirhwng?
Whereareyoubetween?

Organ Yn Dy Geg
Organ in your mouth

Crys Ti
T-shirt or your shirt

Arnofio/Glô in the Dark
Afloat or swimming

Torra Fy Ngwallt Yn Hir
Cut my hair long

Ymaelodi Â'r Ymylon
Joining with the periphery

Pan Ddaw'r Wawr
When the dawn comes

Dacw Hi
There she is

Y Teimlad
The feeling

Ysbeidiau Heulog
Sunny moments

# THANKYOUS

The Furries first agreed to help with this book during a soundcheck in Kentish Town about five years ago. Since then they've gone beyond the call of duty with interviews, coffee rounds, factual corrections and email ramblings – so thanks first and foremost to Gruff, Cian, Daf, Guto and Bunf.

Thanks to my publisher Scott Pack and Rachel Faulkner at The Friday Project for their vision and enthusiasm, and to Pete Fowler for his (inevitably) incredible artwork. Additional interviewees who helped no end include (in no particular order) Dic Ben, Brian Cannon, Gorwel Owen, Alan McGee, Mark James, Emyr Williams, Alan Woodhouse, Dr Kiko and Karen Holzbaur.

Thanks to my good friend Mat Beal for transforming an early draft into something I could present to publishers, and to Melanie Walter and Rhodri Davies for assisting with song title translations. In addition to being interviewed, Karen Holzbaur also did a great job over the years of stoking my enthusiasm.

More generally, salutes to my hometown cronies Oly, Steve, Bagon, Christoph and Tom for getting me into the band over a few games of Mario Kart, to the inhabitants of the Citizens Board including Jonny Abrams, Sarah Soya Bean and Dinx Dinxeh, to Howard Marks, Shan Vahidy, Matt Perrin and the author John

Higgs, who recommended The Friday Project (and also wrote a damn fine book on the KLF).

Finally, big love to Juleigh Collins.